MAKING MANAGEMENT
DEVELOPMENT
STRATEGICALLY EFFECTIVE

Wadenhoe House

MAKING MANAGEMENT DEVELOPMENT STRATEGICALLY EFFECTIVE

Peter D. Hall
Peter W. Norris
Roger Stuart

Published by
The Wadenhoe Centre
in association with

Silver Link Publishing Ltd

First published in September 1995

British Library Cataloguing in Publication Data

A catalogue record for this book is available from the British Library.

ISBN 1 85794 080 6

The Wadenhoe Centre
Wadenhoe House
Nr Oundle
Peterborough PE8 5SS
Tel (01832) 720777
Fax (01832) 720410

Edited, designed and produced by the Book Packaging Department of Silver Link Publishing Ltd
Unit 5, Home Farm Close
Church Street
Wadenhoe
Peterborough PE8 5TE
Tel/fax (01832) 720440

Printed and bound in Great Britain by Biddles Ltd, Guildford, Surrey

ACKNOWLEDGEMENTS

Creating a book like this requires the effort of a team. The authors would like to acknowledge in particular the efforts of three people: Neil Bradley, who has been a source of advice and down-to-earth experience that has enriched the process; Adrienne Birch, who has never allowed our flights of fancy to take over or failed to ensure that our feet were firmly on the ground; and Fay Adams, who has managed the production of the book with good humour and patience. One set of bad handwriting would be sufficient - she has coped with three!

Of course our families and spouses deserve special mention for putting up with the ambitions, despair, dreams and elation - all equally hard to handle. So our thanks go to Margaret, Pam and Chris.

Finally our thanks to all our clients and colleagues without whom we would not have enjoyed the experiences on which the research was based.

CONTENTS

Preface   9

This sets out the initial concerns about the unpredictability of management development outcomes that led to the research project at The Wadenhoe Centre.

Introduction   17

The Introduction outlines the aims, contents and shape of the book. It indicates for whom the book is written and what you should expect from it. It also describes the use of 'snapshots' to illustrate concepts and issues. Each Chapter ends with a checklist of items to be considered at that stage of the development of the Wadenhoe Model for your own organisation.

Chapter 1 Management Development as a Key Strategic Tool   24

At the start of this Chapter it is recognised that organisations need effective managers and that management development is a means to achieve this. To avoid any possible confusion that exists about what constitutes management development, the definition that is used throughout the book is examined here in detail.

Chapter 2 Executive Summary   36

This Chapter is written for the Chief Executive or anyone with similar responsibility. It is an overview of the book and provides an outline explanation of the Wadenhoe Model. It also introduces the idea of Critical Checks for testing the strength of the Model. The final part of the Chapter introduces the Analysis steps for Performance potential, Development needs, 'Place', Process design and Cost Benefit analysis.

Chapter 3 'Creating the Template' - the 5P Platform   **52**

At the start of this Chapter the definition of management development is expanded and the basis for the Wadenhoe Model is set out. The foundation of the Model is the 5P Platform, and each element of this - Performance, Person, Purpose, Process and Place - is explained in detail. The Performance-Development Axis is introduced. The different entry points into the Model are identified and their implications discussed. The Chapter ends by looking at the Strategic Hook upon which the effectiveness of the Model depends.

Chapter 4 'Stacking the Odds for Success' - the Critical Checks   **76**

This Chapter covers the five Critical Checks (the 5 Cs), all of which are concerned with ensuring that the Model is complete in every respect in its assembly, development and application. Critical Checks for Completeness, Content, Connection, Construction and Carrying-Out are all explained here, as are the implications of the Performance-Development Axis (introduced in Chapter 3). The last part of the Chapter recognises the reality of parts of the Model being omitted or the Model being unbalanced or 'skewed'.

**Chapter 5 'The Structure Under the Microscope' -
Platform Content Checks**   **98**

Having reassured ourselves that all the five Ps of the 5P Platform are being considered, the next step is to check on the critical features within each individual P element. This Chapter describes the Critical Content Check that assesses the available information relating to each of the P elements and identifies the need for further information, action and decisions for effective management development.

**Chapter 6 'Inspecting the Rigging' -
Checking the Connections and Cross-bracing**   **123**

So far the book has concentrated on the basic Platform of the Model. How the elements of the Platform are secured together to provide the necessary firmness is covered in this Chapter. Each element is taken and the nature of its Connection with each of the other elements is described. The questions being asked of each Connection are listed.

Chapter 7 'Checking for Seaworthiness' - The Five Analysis Steps   150

By this stage the Model should be well formed. Its completeness has been checked, as has its balance. There are now five further steps of Analysis, and these are described in this Chapter; their purpose is to look at some of the broader interactions to ensure that the parts add up to the whole as envisaged. These Analyses ask questions about the potential for performance, the development needs, the environment in which development is to take place, the design of the development processes and the costs and benefits. Earlier in the Chapter the concept of 'going off-line' is introduced, and the implications of this for each of the Analyses is explained.

Chapter 8 'Launching the Initiative' -
Platform Construction and Carrying-Out Checks   168

This Chapter sets out five Construction Checks that help to ensure that the assembly of the Model is done in a way that predicates for a successful launch. These checks if carried out thoroughly also ensure that the necessary activities take place for maintaining and modifying the Model during and after implementation. We are looking to ensure that any initiative is positioned in the hearts and minds of the participants and other interested parties so that is has a fighting chance of success.

Chapter 9 The Management Development League   183

Here we explore the fact that each organisation has a different starting point and level of sophistication in its development compared with the structure and rigour offered by the Wadenhoe Model. We introduce a League of Management Development and the potential to use the Model as a way of achieving 'promotion' and avoiding 'relegation'.

Chapter 10 Putting a Measure on Management Development   193

The final Chapter looks at the issues involved in trying to improve the quality of evaluation of the real impact of management development. It introduces the next stage of the research process and the potential to link the effort involved in a management development initiative with the bottom-line performance of the organisation.

Appendix 1 Management Development - the Concepts, not the Words   201

Appendix 2 Competence Domains   208

PREFACE

There was not really a shout of 'Eureka'. Nor in the words of the late cricket commentator, Brian Johnston, a 'champagne moment'.

Rather there was a moment when my frustration finally reached a level I could no longer ignore. It also occurred when I had some time to reflect on the nature of my frustrations.

The precise location of this moment was Barcelona. With some 25 colleagues I was taking part in a research conference on management development.

The purpose of the conference was to decide how to allocate a considerable amount of money to research proposals. The money was being put up by a group of international organisations who were concerned that the research that had taken place in the past had not really contributed to the resolution of their problems. Hence their decision to take more control over the placing of major research money. Other participants at the conference represented academic institutions from around the world, invited to submit proposals for research into issues of management and management development that the sponsoring organisations would find valuable.

The morning session had been dedicated to presentations of the proposed research topics. The conference had not yet returned from lunch and therefore the room was quiet. Yet inside I had a feeling of deep disquiet.

My Concerns

So what was the unease and disquiet that I was feeling?

I was conscious of having spent the morning listening to some of the finest academic brains in the field of management development earnestly present their topics for research. My concern centred on why we needed more research into these topics. I felt that we should have reached a stage where these topics were so much part of the way we manage day by day that any further research ought to be redundant.

And yet this clearly was not the case.

It was also a feeling that my chosen profession of management development was at a crossroads, and nothing that I had heard during the morning had reassured me that the direction that it appeared to be taking was one that I wanted to follow.

1   Chiefly therefore there was a feeling of embarrassment that after the expenditure of so much time and effort on management development so little had apparently been accomplished.

The topics for further research were not new. They had been the subject of management development interventions at all levels in organisations. Not only were they on the topic lists of most management development programmes, but also as consultants we had actively worked with organisations to turn the concepts into reality in their own environments. Why were these topics still of concern to the internationally respected businesses represented at this conference? Why had they not become part of the fabric of the way that we manage in our organisations?

So there was a sense almost of dishonesty that clients had spent money on management development that appeared to have paid such a poor return.

Snapshot

At a recent conference of senior managers from a wide range of sectors I suggested from the platform that we were spending about £1bn a year on management development in the UK alone. From my past conversations with Directors and Senior Managers in our major organisations I had concluded that about 75 per cent of that money had been wasted. The sum invested was failing to deliver the change in performance that the organisations required.

The conference thought I was wrong! They concluded that the money was not entirely wasted. It was likely that individually the participants had gained something from their development experiences even if the organisation had not gained significantly. But if the measure was the extent to which the money spent had delivered what the organisations wanted, the amount 'wasted' was closer to 90 per cent!

---

2   There was the frustration at the feeling of deja vu. There have been plenty of conferences held in exotic locations around the world that have looked at the content and processes of management development. What was going to make this one different? Not the academic participants. They, like me, had attended many of the same conferences and were here making these research proposals.

3   I was feeling embarrassed by the displayed values and approaches of many of the practitioners in management development. I have held senior line management positions in organisations, including Board appointments in some of them. My interests had always been in the strategic development of organisations and I hold a strong belief that the success of any organisation and in particular its success in implementing its chosen strategy depends on the quality of its managers.

It was the strength of this conviction that had brought me into management development some ten years earlier, but at that moment I felt that as a management development professional my status and significance was being steadily eroded compared with my roles in the past.

I felt that much of the erosion was being caused by the 'hands off' attitude of many deliverers of management development programmes that was marginalising the importance of their contribution.

So much evaluation of development programmes tests only the reactions of participants to the content and processes of the events to which they have been exposed and, at best, the learning they feel they have gained, that we have been able to justify our activities through the positive noises at the end of a programme. But my concern was with the change in organisational performance that the sponsoring company really wanted. Management development is a means to achieving organisational performance, and we have fallen into the position of treating it as the end itself.

Snapshot

A Professor of a major business school told me that in his view the students on the programme were his only concern. Whether their organisations were in a position to use the learning that he was provoking was not his problem!

---

4   I was feeling embarrassed by the almost blind faith that organisations were placing in the deliverers of management development.

Despite all of the apparent tailoring of management development programmes based on research into the real needs of the organisation, I still felt that, for many of our clients, the decision to invest in a development programme was an 'Act of Faith'. For some the whole process was akin to black magic. Why else would we get such violent reactions to the suggestion that we needed to modify the design to reflect changing needs or to introduce a new face into the delivery team?

Once again our dependence on the type of evaluation mentioned earlier has reinforced this situation. This is often the only 'hard' information available to the client organisation on which to judge the impact of the intervention.

Snapshot

I was recently asked by an international pharmaceutical company to help them to evaluate a £2m management development programme. During the initial meeting they were, however, unable clearly to identify what the programme set out to achieve!

But the feedback from the participants was 'excellent'.

---

5 My frustration was further being fuelled by the knowledge that I had witnessed management development working and achieving the results the organisations wanted with both individuals and the organisation being fulsome in their praise of the contribution the development process had made to the achievement! So it was not a frustration grounded in failure but a frustration of inconsistent and unpredictable success.

Snapshot

One of my colleagues who is a keen amateur golfer points out that it is the occasional brilliant shot that keeps him interested in the game. He knows that he is capable of achieving a great result if only he could repeat the outcome every time. He also recognises, however, that one perfect shot achieved occasionally does not qualify him to become a professional!

Why Me?

I should at this point explain something of my own involvement in management development in order to make sense of my concerns, unease and frustrations.

I have been involved in designing, developing and delivering tailored management development interventions for the past ten years, working with the senior management of some of the most professional organisations in the world. Additionally, I have worked in senior line management positions in engineering organisations and in the service sector.

Each management development intervention in which I have been involved was based on research into the real needs of the organisation and was tailored to achieve a match between their expressed needs and contents and the approach being proposed.

I felt that overall the programmes had been run professionally and had always been well received by the participants who attended and the organisation as a whole who paid the bill.

Many of the colleagues who had worked on the programmes with me over the years had considerable practical experience in their field, usually supported by research, and their experience was thoroughly underpinned by the relevant theories. And what is more, they were usually entertaining!

So my disquiet is built from many years of experience of working with client organisations to try to satisfy their management development needs and not always feeling that the necessary changes in management performance had been achieved.

Why Now?

Just as I finished trying to identify the cause of my unease, the conference delegates filed back for the start of the afternoon session. I really wanted the speakers in the afternoon to reassure me, to excite me, to convince me that as colleagues in my chosen profession they shared my concerns and were thrusting forward to confirm management development as a major strategic tool. I wanted to hear that there really was something new in the research that was being proposed and that it would make the difference we all wanted.

I suppose that if I had been excited and reassured by the afternoon session, our own research would not have been started and this book would never have been written - so I leave you to draw your own conclusions about what happened in the course of that long, warm afternoon.

I found my mind returning to the theme of its earlier musings. This time, though, I started to question why I was feeling this way at this particular time. Was it mere tiredness or was there some substance to my concerns?

A key part of my role at that time was to meet with prospective clients and to understand their needs in a way that would enable me to propose management development activities to meet these needs. It is natural that in those early exchanges with me as a prospective supplier the clients will express the concerns that they have about entering into a management development relationship with me. Of late the concerns had become more strident, more suspicious, more insistent.

- 'Can I trust you with my managers? X down the road sent his managers on a course and they came back with a bunch of fancy ideas that were nothing to do with his business. He ended up losing half of them.'

- 'Why should I spend this money with you when Y appears to be offering to carry out the same work for a fraction of your fees?'

- 'Can't you do it in three days instead of five?'

- 'What is all this going to deliver on my bottom line?'

- 'Do I really need another piece of diagnostic research? Are you implying that we do not understand what is going on in our own business?'

- 'How can I be certain of the impact that this is going to have on the organisation and when will my Directors be able to see the benefits coming through?'

- 'Why should we choose this process for the development? My Director went on an outdoor development course which he thoroughly enjoyed and now he wants everyone to go through the same experience.'

- 'Why do we have to target such a large number of managers? Could we just try a small pilot programme and then see what happens? If the results come through I am sure we could get the budget then to extend it.'

There was no doubt in my mind that a combination of increasing fee rates and the continuing pressure on budgets was adding to the strength of these challenges. The costs of running a development programme at one of the major business schools had more than trebled over the past five years, and in many organisations the decisions that had traditionally been taken by the personnel or training function had moved beyond their normal revenue spending limits into the realms of capital projects.

More decisions were being routed through the purchasing departments, who were concerned with competitive tendering. Investments in management development were being considered alongside major plant purchasing decisions.

I could see little in the economic forecasts that was likely to make significant differences to the pressure on corporate budgets and therefore felt that if I and my colleagues were to retain (or regain) a position of influence in the boardrooms of our client organisations we clearly needed to have some answers to these very understandable and reasonable questions.

And yet part of me also knew that the whole industry of management development was relatively young. In the UK our major business schools are barely thirty years old and only slightly older in the United States.

Was then the cause of my concerns a natural 'coming of age' as I travelled through adolescence in my profession and started to worry about what the future might hold? Was I questioning what I wanted to be when I grew up? This is certainly another factor, like the economic climate, that has combined to add to the pressure to live up to expectations.

Just as we look with tolerance, amusement and pride on the achievements of our children as they grow, there comes a time in the eyes of even the most indulgent of parents when we look for some signs of growing responsibility. Management development has enjoyed all the arrogance, energy and irreverence of youth. It has demanded that we think differently about the processes of development as opposed to training. Now it is time to see the responsibility and professionalism emerge that will transform the gangling youth into a mature and respected figure. The alternative of degeneration into the commercial equivalent of a New Age Traveller is beyond contemplation.

I would like to be able to claim that there was a sudden flash of inspiration that led me to the answer to these questions.

There was not.

However, I did leave the conference with a determination to share my concerns with a number of like-minded colleagues to see whether the collected wisdom of their hundred years or more of management development experience would shed some light on the subject.

One Month Later

The conference had ended without adding any further insights to make my concerns less relevant, and I had returned to the UK with a list of my frustrations and concerns written on the back of the conference programme - and the germ of an idea.

It took me a month to fight my way clear of the work that had built up during the time at the conference and to find a date when I could sit down with a few close colleagues to express my doubts.

The elapsed time was useful because I found reassurance that the concerns felt just as real and important after a month as they had done in Barcelona - too often the 'brilliant' idea dulls in the face of reality.

Each of the three colleagues I had selected had considerably more experience of management development than I, and were all actively involved in running research programmes in management development. I knew from other conversations that they felt some of the same frustrations, but I was not sure how strong their feelings of embarrassment and failure went.

Peter Norris I have known and worked with over many years. A recognised expert in the design of management development initiatives, Peter's practical experience with Michelin and Shell is combined with an incisive brain and many years experience as a consultant.

Dr Roger Stuart has long experience of management development and is widely recognised as one of the leading authorities in the field. He has considerable experience and skill in bridging between the worlds of academic theory and commercial practise. I knew that Roger would be a creative and analytical contributor to the research.

The third member was Neil Bradley. An independent consultant for many years, Neil has 'sharp end' experience of management development from supervisory level to the boardroom and brings an earthy pragmatism to our discussions.

That initial meeting was lively. Not because we disagreed in principle, but because we all recognised that there were successes as well as failures to be considered. Management development is not a complete black hole of failure.

What is more, our experience was not limited to the delivery of management development 'courses'. We had ranged across the extremes of management development interventions as consultants, trainers, in-company organisation development practitioners and as line managers.

We spent that initial day trying to test for the differences between the interventions that had delivered and those that had not. If, as I held, 75 per cent of management development effort was ineffective, what was it that made the other 25 per cent work in the way that it should? We searched our experiences for the 'magic ingredient' that we could add.

The conclusion from that day was not that management development did not work, but that it clearly did. *The issue was that it did not work often enough or predictably enough for us to be satisfied with our professional status.*

Having shared our concerns about management development and having confirmed that the feelings that had run through me in Barcelona were not unique, we had to ask the question 'So what?'. Were we looking for the impossible? At the end of the day did it matter? Should we just sit tight and hope for a return to the 'demand exceeds supply' situation that had existed in the recent past? What, if anything, were we willing to do about it?

Righteous indignation aside, were we willing to put our money where our mouths were and work together in pooling our experience and time to look for an answer to our shared concerns?

You are reading our answer.

Peter David Hall
Managing Director
The Wadenhoe Centre
June 1995

INTRODUCTION

What is This Book About?

This is a book about improving your organisation's profits. The safety and well-being of your organisation's profits are under the control of your managers and leaders. Up to and including the board. If they do not possess the necessary skills, knowledge and outlook to create and sustain a competitive position for the organisation, the ability to deliver the added value that the marketplace expects could be severely compromised.

This is a book about determining ways for increasing the effectiveness of how we develop our managerial resources in order to capture and sustain that competitive advantage. That is why it is a book about profits.

It is not a cook book with lots of preferred recipes. Neither is it a 'knocking' book in which we seek to denigrate other ideas in favour of our own.

Rather it is a 'drawing together' book in which we seek to make sense of the mass of often conflicting views and ideas for increasing the effectiveness of management development activities.

And finally it is a book about investment. Management development is a legitimate business investment aimed at improving the productivity of a crucial resource. As such we should be able to identify clearly the return that we expect and to measure the resulting gain from that investment. This book looks at how we can more comfortably view management development as an investment rather than as a pure cost.

Who Should Read It?

Top managers, Directors and owners who have a stake in the commercial success of their organisations *must* be concerned with management development. At the very least they will be aware that the real cost of management development has increased steadily over recent years and will be feeling the pressure to increase the benefits that they are able to identify in terms of improvements in their organisation's competitive performance.

Equally it is aimed at those HR and management development specialists who are charged with ensuring that their organisation always has the right managerial capabilities for the direction it wants to take.

This is a book, therefore, written for top management as well as the management development and HR specialists.

Recognising that the most senior people may not at this stage wish to immerse themselves in the full detail of how to make Management Development Strategically Effective, Chapter 2 is written as an Executive Overview. Senior managers may choose then to read further or decide to pass the book on to their management development professionals.

The Aims of the Book

We would not be true to our canons if at the outset we did not make clear what the book is intended to achieve. We believe that by the end of the book you should:

● Understand why management development is a key and vital strategic tool

● Understand the elements of the Wadenhoe Model and how these provide a framework for thinking about management development

● Have tested the elements of the Wadenhoe Model against your own experience and current management development activities

● Understand how the thinking in the Wadenhoe Model would increase the effectiveness of management development in your organisation

● Have a framework for analysing the Present State and Desired State of Performance in your organisation as a basis for defining development needs

● Understand the steps to be taken to implement Strategically Effective Management Development interventions

● Understand how to maintain the currency of the Model as a strategic tool.

How to Use the Book

If you wish, you could read the book all the way through before you start any analysis. However, we believe that it is more likely that you will want to build up your familiarity with the tools as we go through in order to make more sense of the ideas that are introduced later.

The core of this book therefore is a rigorous framework for examining and improving the strategic effectiveness of management development. Through working with the framework with rigour in the context of your organisation you will be increasing the impact of both your management development strategy and the specific interventions.

We start with some scene-setting in Chapter 1 in which we will look at why we believe management development needs to be strategic. We will ask you at this point to look at your own organisation to see to what extent the strategic links that we identify are in place and effective.

As we have mentioned, Chapter 2 is written as an Executive Overview. In it we will introduce you to the Wadenhoe Model, the framework around which this book is built. This framework has emerged from The Wadenhoe Centre research over the past two years and has been extensively tested with our own client organisations.

THE WADENHOE MODEL
is
a framework or organiser for thinking and action in
PLANNING,
DESIGNING
and
DELIVERING
MANAGEMENT DEVELOPMENT INITIATIVES

By the end of Chapter 2 you should have sufficient understanding of the Model and what it can do for you to be willing to undertake the work that is involved in working through the Model in the remainder of the book.

In Chapters 3 to 8 we say to the management development professional, 'We are now out of the boardroom; it is time to take your jacket off and really get to work to understand the Model and to make it work for you.'

Chapter 9 provides a way for benchmarking your own organisation's management development against the Model in a manner that provides some insights into the way forward. A form of 'League Table' is offered against which you can position your own organisation - and any other with which you are sufficiently familiar.

We have said from the outset that we see management development as an investment. No organisation makes significant investment decisions without a clear idea of the benefits to be gained from the investment. In addition many organisations are required to review formally the extent to which the investment has actually delivered the anticipated benefits. In Chapter 10 we explain the next stage of our research into 'Putting a Measure on Management Development'.

The 'Snapshots'

In each of the chapters we will provide illustrations from our own experience of how issues appear in other organisations. We call these 'snapshots' - how things were in an organisation at a particular time. In each case one of our team has first-hand knowledge of the circumstances in a snapshot and the wider organisation in which it is set. Here is an example of a snapshot; this one is longer than most that appear later since it covers a range of the type of management development issues that the use of the Model is bound to cause to surface and lay bare for examination. We say 'lay bare' since we know that decisions about management development are not always made objectively. They can be clouded by company politics, power games, personal preference and so on.

Snapshot

The senior management of an engineering company with worldwide operations became concerned about the identification and development of its managerial talent. Over the years piecemeal development activities had taken place in the group of which the company was part. Now it had changed ownership. The board commissioned external consultants to design and run Assessment Centres for those managerial employees who might have potential for further development and promotion. They also commissioned other consultants to run a programme of outdoor training for the same target group. There were sufficient managers for these activities to be run several times a year.

A particular group of managers became very negative after the Assessment Centre. Each thought that he or she had been lowly rated on factors that to them (and, in some cases, to the executives to whom they reported) seemed irrelevant for their performance now or in the immediate future.

Because of this they also had serious doubts about the value of attending the outdoor programme. They then found that the criteria and behaviours against which they had been assessed were based on generalised research by consultants, the appropriateness and applicability of which had never been tested in their company. The criteria had been approved by the senior executives of the company after a presentation by the consultants.

It leaked out during a training session that the company had succession

Continued on next page

Continued from previous page

plans for managers. None of this group of managers knew that these existed and, naturally, did not know what effect these were likely to have on their futures.

Trying to redress the negative effect of these factors on this group of managers consumed hundreds of managerial hours and the hasty introduction of remedial actions, which, while acting as palliatives, did little for the credibility of development in that company.

The Wadenhoe Model is a Framework

Throughout this book we will refer to the Model as a 'framework', as an 'organiser for your thoughts'. The ideal framework is:

- Generaliseable across different contexts
- Simple, ie comprehensible
- Accurate.

Unfortunately in the real world we face the dilemma that only two out of these three ideals are achievable at any one time. The work of Warren Thorngate in the 1970s was developed by Roger Stuart and suggests that any framework or model may be:

- **generaliseable** and **simple**, but **inaccurate**, ie at best an approximation to the truth, so runs the risk of being perceived as interesting but not relevant to us

- **simple** and **accurate**, but **specific**; such frameworks may well be viewed as relevant and usable in the context of one organisation, but of limited repeatability or applicability elsewhere

- **generaliseable** and **accurate**, but **complex**, ie difficult to understand, so may be judged as impressive but impractical, so fuelling user-resistance.

In proposing our Model we have had to accept these constraints and make some choices. We have chosen therefore to make the Model **generaliseable** and **simple**. In doing so we face the risk that it might be seen as not being accurate - not accurate, that is, in the context of your specific organisation and circumstances.

In writing this book therefore we do not pretend to provide instant solutions. We have, instead, written a book that will require that you use the frameworks to draw the appropriate conclusions for your organisation. We will continuously draw your attention to the areas where you will need to apply the frameworks to your own analysis and provide guidelines for how to do this. It is this process of 'Contextualisation' that will then make the Model **accurate**, **simple** and **specific**.

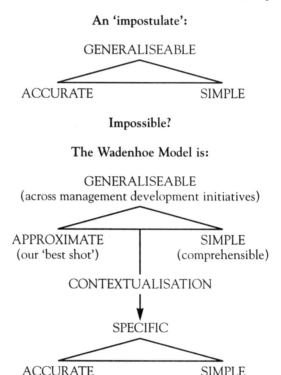

An 'impostulate':

GENERALISEABLE

ACCURATE   SIMPLE

Impossible?

The Wadenhoe Model is:

GENERALISEABLE
(across management development initiatives)

APPROXIMATE   SIMPLE
(our 'best shot')   (comprehensible)

CONTEXTUALISATION

SPECIFIC

ACCURATE   SIMPLE

What Should you Expect from this Book?

The focus of the book is, as the title suggests, 'Making Management Development Strategically Effective'. This is the sort of book title that gives the marketing people nightmares - but it is what the book is all about!

The concerns that were expressed in the Preface are centred around the unpredictability of the outcomes of management development efforts. We believe that this book will provide you with the frameworks for increasing the rigour that you apply to your management development thinking and thereby increase the predictability of the outcomes.

We believe that the overall result of working through this book should be that you will be:

● Able consistently to achieve the development of the long-term performance of managers in your organisation in the most cost-effective manner and to a standard that will enable them to deliver the declared strategy of the organisation.

Perhaps an appropriate way to round off this Introduction is through another snapshot:

Snapshot

A Personnel Director recently told us: 'Until about ten years ago we had many management development activities. And then the Finance Director started asking the impossible-to-answer question: 'What has all this added to the bottom line?' No one was able to give him a satisfactory answer, and from then the activities dwindled to the extent that we are doing nothing now. The view of top management was that we had been successful doing what we had always done. No one seemed to make a positive decision about this. It just happened.

But this is not going to see us through the massive changes that our industry is facing.'

Chapter 1
MANAGEMENT DEVELOPMENT AS A KEY STRATEGIC TOOL

'... there are certain things which absolutely must be achieved if the business is to survive, grow and be profitable. The organisational capability to achieve these critical success factors is a result of the management capability of the firm'.

Alan Sugar, Chairman, Amstrad

The Need for Effective Managers

Senior industrialists of the calibre of Alan Sugar identify that the long-term strategic success of the organisation will come only through the capability of its managers. On the other hand, we are apparently not achieving the development results that we require through our traditional management development approaches. All the evidence points to there being a widespread inconsistency in thinking about management development.

The nature of comments made to us illustrate this:

- 'You can't teach managers; they are born with it. You only have to look at the great leaders like Churchill - he never went on any management training programmes.'

- 'We sent one of our people to a course at X. Came back with his head full of theoretical nonsense. Utterly useless. He could not apply it and in the end we let him go. Total waste of money.'

- 'We enjoyed ourselves but the tutor really did not have a clue. He did not understand our business so we had to try to understand what managing in ICI had to do with us. He was a Professor so he should have been good, but he had never had a proper job in his life.'

- 'We were out all night tramping around the countryside and I am still not sure what we learned from it other than the sadistic nature of the tutor.'

- 'I learned a great deal about how to run a business properly, but I get no chance to use it in my present job.'

- 'I wanted to start my own business so when the company sent me on this course I thought "Great - I will learn as much as I can even though I will never have the chance to use it in this company".'

- 'It helped me to realise what a shambles we are in, so as soon as I had the chance I moved to another organisation that was in better shape.'

- 'I enjoyed the programme but I still do not know why I was sent on it. It really had no relevance for my job. I can only conclude that we had paid for the place and the proper participant dropped out at the last minute.'

- 'I thought the course was about team building, my boss thought it was about improving my interpersonal skills and the tutor was into self-awareness.'

- 'When I was sent on the programme I wondered what I had done wrong. When I returned and they promoted me I was absolutely amazed.'

- 'I am financially illiterate and just wanted to understand the company's budgeting system. But some of the others wanted to look at gearing and stock market flotations. I found it an absolute nightmare.'

- 'We spent £2m on this development programme with a leading business school and now the Chairman wants me to evaluate it. I thought that he understood that it was a long-term education process.'

- 'We sent everyone on a lateral thinking programme but we are still not seeing any action in our Quality Circles.'

- 'We can no longer afford for management development to be an act of faith. We have got to be able to demonstrate the benefits.'

- 'There is no personnel team left any more - just me. So I cannot afford the time to help 15 different consultants learn about the organisation in order to be effective.'

- 'Buying a course is not a problem. Achieving real development is something completely different.'

- 'Filling their heads with unrealistic expectations is useless to me. I need some-one who will understand our value system and work with us within that.'

Patently, there is much to be found in organisations that travels under the name of management development but which is not connected to the business strate-gy and in many cases lacks defined purpose or even sound design. This, we sub-mit, is the waste of money signalled in the Preface to this book.

Perhaps we ought to start with what one of our colleagues calls 'GOBO' - a Glimpse Of the Blindingly Obvious!

'Organisations do not want management development'

In some ways this is like the flash of inspiration that led Black & Decker to realise that their customers do not want to buy a drill! What they really want is a hole somewhere, or even more fundamentally they may just want something attached to a wall. Unfortunately they have discovered that they cannot go into their local hardware store and buy a bag of holes, and therefore buying a drill is the only alternative (at present!).

So it is with management development. Businesses do not want management development programmes - they want effective managers.

And even this assertion needs to be challenged. At the end of the day the aim of most businesses is to achieve long-term competitive performance and the financial results that their shareholders are expecting. Managers are a means to achieving this end. So we can go as far as defining management development as a means to a means to an end!

If we accept that the creation of strategically effective managers is the aim of man-agement development, let us examine the other side of the coin, ie how do we ensure that our management development activities properly meet the strategic needs of the organisation? How do we make management development a key strategic tool?

All of these comments and observations raise a number of issues:

- Is there a clear and shared understanding of what we mean by management development? Where are the distinctions, for example, between career planning, personal development and other activities that often share this same banner?

● Do organisations have a clear view of what their investment in management development is trying to achieve and the return that they expect from their investment?

● Are the objectives of a management development initiative defined with sufficient clarity and purpose before an initiative is given the go-ahead?

● Is there objective information available to evaluate what has actually been achieved before we dismiss management development as a waste of time?

Obviously there are alternatives to management development as a way of ensuring that we have managers with the right capabilities. We can, for example, buy in managers with the skills that we require and discard those who are obsolete or not performing. In general, however, there are insufficient 'born leaders' to go round, so development again comes into consideration.

But let us return to our original theme. We want effective managers who will deliver the long-term strategic aims of the organisation. But traditionally the money that we have spent on developing these managers has not delivered what the organisation feels that it needs.

What is Management Development?

Before we went too far into the research we came up against the obvious question: 'Just what do we mean by management development?'

Over recent years the number of terms that are used to describe management development and its elements has increased dramatically, leaving people confused and unclear. Management training? Manager development? Management development? Personal development? These and many other terms are being used, sometimes loosely and frequently interchangeably.

Snapshot

A manager attending a general management course at a business school found herself on the top of a hill, cold and wet, in the middle of the night doing things for which she could see neither the purpose nor relevance to her role in a financial services company in the City of London. Later, during a review of what had happened, she found herself challenged

Continued on next page

Continued from previous page

aggressively in the public gaze of the twenty other members of the course by one of the tutors about the way she had handled the situation. Before entering this module she had received no briefing from her company other than 'Go along and enjoy it: everyone else has'. Other than generalised statements by the tutors, no explanation of what the module offered had been given. She felt humiliated and spent the rest of the time avoiding being in a position to be attacked again. On returning to her company there was no further debriefing.

Unfortunately, this individual is not unique in what she experienced.

Was the purpose personal development or manager development? By our definition it certainly wasn't management development, and we are not convinced that it was developmental for managerial skills!

Do we always know which we mean? And does it matter anyway?

Of course it does! This confusion of language and definitions has serious implications for all of us who are concerned with management development. In the Appendix we have included some definition of these various terms, from a paper that was first published in our 'Occasional Paper' series.

Snapshot

We know of organisations that are encouraging their managers and other employees to carry out Personal Development Planning. Yet the management of these organisations have not made their intentions clear about the purposes of these within the HR scheme of things. Nor has the nature of this development process been fully described, and as a result expectations that are not likely to be met have been raised. These are not necessarily expectations of promotion but expectations that line managers and others will *willingly* and *enthusiastically* contribute to this development process. The enthusiasm of the HR people for Personal Development Planning is not mirrored by line management. Confusion in these circumstances has left frustration and cynicism, which are not good foundations on which to build constructive development processes.

It is not surprising that companies have this problem when even our leading business schools are not clear in which fields of development their programmes are operating. Examine the promotional literature of most business schools and you will find a seemingly random use of terms. For the purpose of this book we propose the following definition of management development:

> # MANAGEMENT DEVELOPMENT IS
> # A PLANNED AND PURPOSEFUL PROCESS
> # FOR ENABLING MANAGERS' PERFORMANCE
> # IN THEIR PLACE OF WORK

'A Planned and Purposeful Process for enabling managers' Performance in their Place of work.' It is within this definition that we look to find the answers to our original question: 'How do we make management development a key strategic tool?'

'Performance'

As our approach to the development of corporate and business strategies for our organisations becomes more professional and more comprehensive, we are also starting to recognise the change of vocabulary in the field of strategy. We now talk of 'strategic thinking' as opposed to strategic planning. We are increasingly focusing on the issues of implementation of strategy rather than limiting our thinking to formulation only.

With these changes, and with the acceptance of managerial performance as a key factor in our ability to implement strategy successfully, has come increasing pressure to be clear about what we require of our managers. What is the 'Performance' that is required in order to give life to our strategic ambitions? We often define jobs in terms of the inputs that are required and the tasks that must be done. The challenge in many of our organisations is to define without any ambiguity the output that we must have from each managerial role if we are to deliver a long-term competitive performance from the organisation.

It follows that without a clear specification of the managerial performance required, we are unable to appraise that performance purposefully. Further, our ability to measure the achievement of our management development activities must also be severely limited.

The definition of the Performance that is required of our managers by the corporate and business strategies of our organisations is at the core of making management development a key strategic tool.

'Planned'

We are looking here for the conscious planning and preparation that will increase the strategic effectiveness of our management development actions.

Just as the great military strategists rate success as '90 per cent perspiration and 10 per cent inspiration', so we recognise that there will be opportunities to learn and develop that are unplanned and inspirational.

But we would also subscribe to the view of Louis Pasteur that 'Chance favours only the mind that is prepared'. Opportunism depends on recognising opportunities for what they are whenever they occur. This is the concept of 'emergent planning'. It is acceptable that with a clear sense of direction we fully expect to refine and even redraw our plans on the basis of what we have found or learned.

'Planned' is the word used in our definition, but the realities of organisational life will mean that there will be much unplanned and less than deliberate activity in practical management development. This should not be excluded, provided that it fits within the overall strategic intention of the organisation. Unplanned, therefore, must not mean unrecognised! There is much to be said for assuming and encouraging it to happen.

'Purposeful Process'

We are defining the need for management development to be a 'Purposeful Process'. We have already looked at the need for organisations to define the Performance that they require from their managers. Here we are looking for them to define the performance that they require of any selected development process.

Our research shows that companies respond to the brochures of management courses without necessarily knowing much more about the content than the list of short subject headings provided by the supplier. More importantly, they often make their choices without understanding or questioning the processes that the course delegates will encounter and whether this is appropriate for the learning and development that they require.

For there to be an informed choice of an effective learning or development process and the evaluation of development activities there must be clearly understood outcomes or purposes.

Current thinking demands a sharper and more strategic view of management development than the educational or training view. The funding of employees to take MBA degrees, sending all managers to a business school for a general management course, training managers in appraisal skills - these are only valid if they are part of a planned effort to sustain the strategy of the organisation.

'Enabling managers' performance'

Perhaps the interesting aspect of this part of the definition is when we try to identify what *disables* managers from performing in the way and to the standard that is required. Just as our understanding of motivation recognises the impact of 'de-motivators', if we are to increase the impact of our management development initiatives in terms of managerial performance, we will also need to look at the issues that prevent it. In this we are assuming that we have managers who are capable of performing in the desired way and to the required standard.

To make our management development initiatives strategically effective, therefore, we may also need to develop the environment in which the managerial performance is delivered.

'Place of work'

The performance that we require of managers to deliver the organisation's long-term strategic ambitions is the performance that takes place at work. We can all behave as different people at home, on the club committee or on the training programme. The issue for management development is the performance that is exhibited at work.

Management development is not solely concerned with management training, coaching, mentoring, action learning and other techniques. These are the *mechanisms* for learning how to perform as managers, but their use does not necessarily transform managerial performance.

Without appropriate structures - including the way teams are constituted and used, systems for performance management, reward and control, approaches for identifying and selecting people for management, etc - the learning may not have the opportunity to be transferred and take root in the organisation.

Snapshot

A newly appointed management development adviser in the production division of a large, conglomerate company counted the number of days spent by managers on training. This amounted to a very considerable opportunity cost in addition to the substantial course, accommodation and subsistence fees. The reactions of participants to the training were unanimous that it was 'very good'. But he could find no connection between the training undertaken and the company's business plans, and there was no obvious link between this cost and any improvement in the company's performance.

He therefore suspended all management training, but only until every manager at the most senior levels had undertaken training themselves in how to determine training and development needs that would actually *enhance the achievement of their own business plans and support the implementation of future strategy*. This specific skills training for senior managers was also aimed at improving their own capability for talking with those managers who had attended training to see how the learning could be applied to the achievement of the business plans.

Management Development as a Key Strategic Tool

Let us then return to the definition of management development that we proposed.

'A Planned and Purposeful Process for enabling managers' Performance in their Place of work'

For management development to be a key strategic tool, therefore, we must be looking at:

- A clear understanding of the managerial performance that the strategy will require both now and in the future

- An understanding of the range of development and learning processes that are available

- The intention to manage actively the range of development processes and opportunities

- Clear definitions of what each development intervention is required to deliver

- The ability to understand and influence the factors that can disable a manager from performing in the desired way

- A recognition and acceptance that development has not occurred until there is a change in managerial performance at work.

The Wadenhoe Model
for achieving more strategically effective management development
is
ESSENTIALLY PRAGMATIC
INSTRUMENTAL
(a means to a means to an end!)
INTEGRATED AND INTEGRATEABLE
GENERALISEABLE
SIMPLE
(but not simplistic)

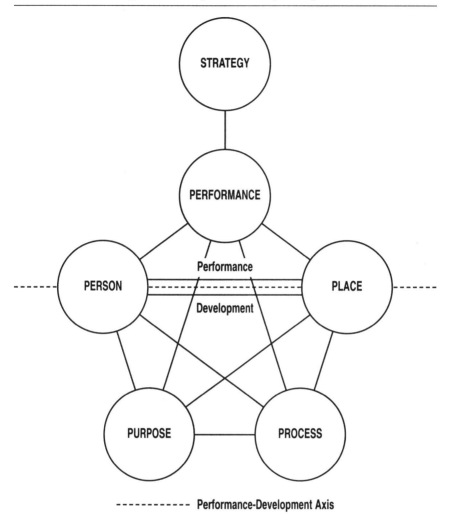

The Wadenhoe Model

Summary

Once again there are no lights flashing or bells ringing as a result of thinking about what we need to do to make management development a key strategic tool. Neither is there any real argument about why we need our managers to perform if our business is to achieve long-term success.

The answers are obvious. Why then doesn't our practice readily demonstrate our grasp of these issues and their means of resolution?

We believe that the reason lies in the lack of an adequate framework that will enable us, rigorously and effectively, to seek, process and make decisions on information relating to the key factors involved in successful management development initiatives.

The aim of the rest of this book is to remedy this shortfall by presenting just such a framework - the Wadenhoe Model.

Checklist for Chapter 1

● In your organisation is management development regarded as a means to the improvement of strategic business performance rather than being an end in itself?

● What is your understanding of the differences between management development, manager development, personal development, career development and management training? Is that understanding of the differences shared with your Board and line management?

● In your organisation is management development seen as an investment? If so, is there a shared understanding of the expected return from the investment? If it is not seen as an investment but only as a cost, what are the implications of this?

● Do your management development initiatives have clear objectives that are written and agreed with line managers before the initiatives are given the go-ahead?

● Does your organisation carry out formal reviews of the management development activities to test whether the objectives have been met and whether the returns on the investment have actually been achieved?

● What is done to track the impact of your management development actions over time?

● How clear is your understanding of the business strategy that your management development actions are trying to affect?

● How does the environment in your organisation enable or disable the managerial performance that is required? Do you take this factor into account when planning for management development?

● How well does your organisation recognise, acknowledge and encourage 'unplanned' development?

- Management development can only be judged to be effective when there is a change in managerial performance at work. How does this fit in with your beliefs about management development? To what extent is this a consideration when you are planning management development?

- Do you recognise the range of development methods that are available to you? (You might like to list those currently in use in your organisation and reflect on what this tells you.)

Chapter 2
EXECUTIVE SUMMARY

Introduction

The vision that drove us to carry out the research that led to this book was of management development making a crucial contribution to the achievement of an organisation's strategic aims and objectives.

Our experience shows us that this is an achievable vision. We have all worked with organisations on particular development activities that have made a measurable and positive impact on that organisation's success - an impact that has been acknowledged by all concerned as crucial to the delivery of the strategy.

Equally, we are aware that this positive impact is not achieved consistently or predictably enough for us to say that our vision is the reality. We therefore used the research to identify the key reasons why management development was so apparently 'hit and miss'.

Some of the reasons were:

- Lack of clarity about what the development should really be achieving

- Inability to handle the volume of data that needed to be considered in making management development decisions

- Biased thinking about particular tools and techniques of management development

- Uncertainty about the strategy of the organisation that management development was trying to affect

- Lack of understanding of the range of processes that were available to achieve management development

- Poor definition of the management performance that any development activity should address

- Inadequate understanding of the impact of the environment at work on the development process

- Incomplete or biased information used for decision-making about management development.

Overall, we concluded that management developers lacked a framework, an organiser for their thoughts that would help them to handle the volume of often conflicting information available in a way that improved the quality of the decisions they were making. At the same time a framework was needed that would apply a sense of rigour to the thinking.

We also concluded that there was no 'magic ingredient' that we had somehow overlooked. There was no 'quick fix' that could be applied to our existing thinking that would in some way make the difference.

We concluded that all the ingredients existed for management development success. The issue was the lack of an effective recipe. The outcome from the research, therefore, was the development of a framework to allow the necessary rigour to be applied. The framework that we developed we have called the Wadenhoe Model.

In this Executive Summary we aim to provide you with an understanding of the way that the Wadenhoe Model works as an organiser for our management development thinking and effective action. In Chapter 1 we made the case for management development to be a key strategic tool; we will show here how the Model helps to make that crucial link into the strategic thinking of the organisation.

The rest of this book looks at the Model in much more detail, asks some key questions and challenges the way that you currently approach management development.

The Wadenhoe Model

To reveal fully the Wadenhoe Model we will etch away at the surface of your thinking.

Our research identified that there are five essential elements that cover all those aspects of an organisation and its strategy that should inform our management development thinking. We have chosen to give each of these elements a title word beginning with the letter 'P', and the combination of these five elements is what we have defined as the **5P Platform** of the Model, as seen in the diagram below.

The five elements are **Performance, Person, Purpose, Process** and **Place.**

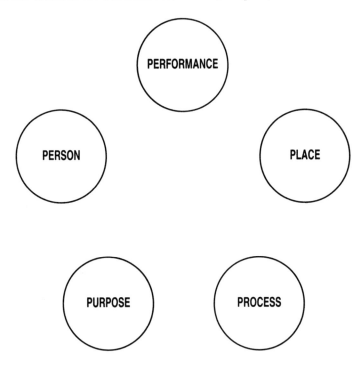

Performance

We believe that it is fundamental to any successful management development intervention that we have a clear understanding of the managerial Performance that we are trying to affect.

In turn, the definition of that Performance is wholly dependent on the strategy of the organisation and how its managers will need to contribute to the achievement of the strategy. And yet a definition of Performance is often not readily available, nor is a clear understanding of the strategic ambitions of the organisation.

The Wadenhoe Model demands that we consider the existing Performance of the organisation's managers and compare this with the Performance that the strategy requires.

Person
The second P on our 5P Platform is the P of Person.

The people who we are considering for development are your managers, with all their skills and enthusiasms, their experiences and their foibles, their blindspots and their prejudices. This is the base on which any change in managerial performance is to be built. Without an understanding of the current capabilities and characteristics of each of the managers to be involved in the planned development process we could be making assumptions that are simply not valid.

Purpose
The third P is the P of Purpose.

Can we define precisely the development objectives that the planned programme of management development activities has to achieve? We have accepted the value of using objectives to manage performance in most aspects of our working lives - why not in management development?

Within the Wadenhoe Model we believe that it is essential to be able to define the development objectives if we are to move towards strategically effective management development.

Process
The fourth P of our 5P Platform is the P of Process.

Management development is about learning. Andrej Huczinski identifies over 300 methods for learning in his *Encyclopaedia of Learning Methods*. And yet when it comes to management development we seem to think in very narrow terms about development processes. All too often the thinking appears to be limited to a course or some 'flavour of the month' approach.

The power of the Wadenhoe Model is not in rubbishing particular development processes that do not match our prejudices. The power of the Model is in demanding recognition of alternative methods of development. It requires that we consider these alternatives and make some decisions about the most effective process for achieving the declared development objectives that will improve the performance that is required from this particular set of managers.

Place
The final P in the 5P Platform is the P of Place.

By Place we mean the environment in which both the development and, more importantly, the Performance will be required to happen. For example, the venue in which a particular development event is to be delivered is one aspect of Place.

Often in our experience the appropriateness of the venue receives scant consideration compared with the availability of leisure facilities!

However, the more important aspect of the environment for learning concerns the workplace. One of our strong values is that development has not taken place until there is a change in behaviour and performance at work. An obvious implication of this is that as a recognised and accepted part of the development process the manager will be doing some experimentation at work with the new ideas.

What happens in your organisation to people who try things that don't work first time? In some organisations this is not a pleasant experience. In one organisation I visited recently my contact said, 'You only experiment here after you have got another job!' The likely enthusiasm for on-the-job learning or the impact of an extensive development programme is not going to be great!

Therefore, part of our consideration of Place is the extent to which the environment at work is supportive of the learning process.

The other part of the consideration is the extent to which the environment at work encourages people actually to perform in the way that is being defined.

Thus when we talk about Place in the context of the Wadenhoe Model these are the issues that we are considering - the environment for development and for performance.

Snapshot

I was asked by one of our premier engineering companies to make their senior managers 'more entrepreneurial'. What they really wanted was for people to take more risks. As we talked with the managers involved we quickly learned that their only concern with taking risks was the verbal flogging that the Managing Director administered to the last person who took a risk that did not work!

And then they wondered why people were not willing to take risks.

These then are the five elements that combine to make our 5P Platform.

'So what?' I hear you exclaim. The who, what, why, where and when of management development. We agree. But like the creation of a great painting, it is not the tubes of primary colours that make the work of art, but the quality of the ingredients and colours and the way that they are blended, interconnected, shaded and counterbalanced. So it is with the Wadenhoe Model.

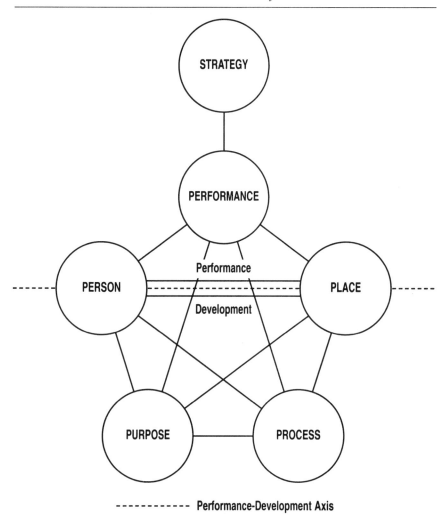

---------- **Performance-Development Axis**

The 5 Cs

From this initial identification of the essential ingredients of management development we looked at how they need to be combined to create the required result. Thus the strength of the Wadenhoe Model is in what we have termed the Critical Checks, or 'Cs'. Again there are five of these and they conform to the process of etching away at our thinking.

Our **5 Cs** or **Critical Checks** are as follows:

Platform Completeness Check
Are all the P elements of Performance, Person, Purpose, Process and Place appropriately and intentionally in place?

Platform Content Check

Have the critical ingredients of each of the P elements been identified?

Platform Connection Check

Are the elements of the Model - the 5Ps - systematically and compatibly linked into a cohesive whole?

Platform Construction Check

Has the Model been assembled in a way that predicates for a successful launch?

Platform Carrying-Out Check

Have the necessary steps been taken to maintain and modify the Model in implementation?

Let us look at each of these in a little more detail.

The first C is the **Critical Check for Platform Completeness**. We have observed organisations in the research where one or more of the elements that make up the 5P Platform is missing from their management development thinking. We found organisations where, for example, the P of Purpose was completely missing. In other words the organisation was actively prosecuting management development initiatives for which no development objectives had been defined.

In others the P of Person was missing. Here development programmes were being run that everyone had to attend irrespective of need or appropriateness.

These omissions led to the thinking about management development in some way being incomplete in those organisations.

A further dimension of the Check for Platform Completeness was where we observed an imbalance in the importance that the organisation placed on one or other of the P elements. Thus, although all the elements of our 5P Platform appeared to be present the thinking was skewed by the dominance of one of the elements.

For example, we observed organisations where the P of Process dominated the thinking. The organisation strongly favoured one particular process and it was used for all forms of development. We have seen this in the case of action learning, computer-based training, MBAs and outdoor development. But of course the strongest form of bias has been towards the good old 'course'. We still hear managers in organisations protesting that they have not received any development this year because they have not been on a course.

Having done our first etch of the surface to reveal the existence and relative size of each of the elements, the next etch is to see what exists inside each of the elements. This is the **Critical Check for Platform Content**.

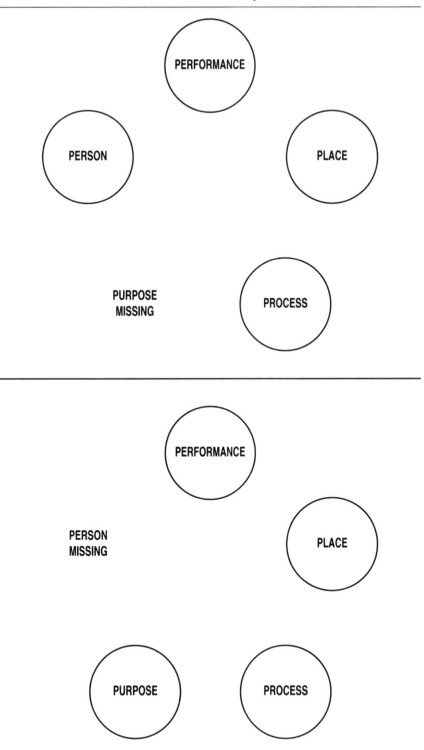

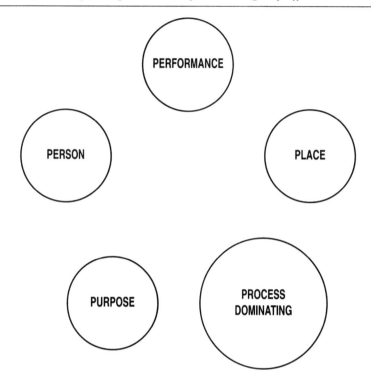

We have developed check lists to help us to identify the vital and critical information that must exist inside each of the P elements. For example, as we look at the P of Performance we are asking whether the key performance areas are clearly identified and articulated for the roles that are being considered. We are asking whether there is quality information available on how each of the potential participants is currently performing against the criteria that have been established.

And so on around the five elements of the Model.

It is at this stage that we also identify another aspect of the Model that our etching process has revealed. As was touched on above, the elements of Person and Place each have two dimensions.

When we are considering the Person who is to be developed we are concerned with understanding the Competencies and Characteristics of that individual that impact both on their willingness and ability to Perform and on their willingness and ability to Develop. Similarly, when we look at the element of Place we are concerned with understanding the impact of the environment on the individual's willingness and ability to Perform and to Develop.

So we have identified the existence of an Axis that runs across the Model through the elements of Person and Place. We call this the Performance-Development Axis.

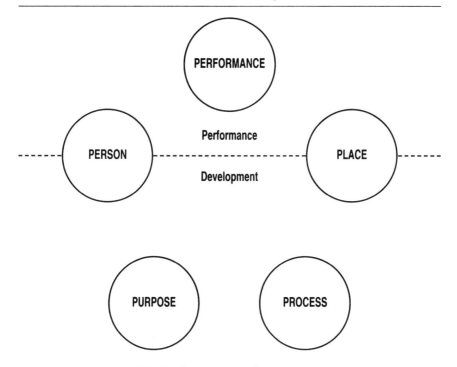

The Performance-Development Axis

Above the Axis we are concerned with considerations related to Performance, while below the Axis we are concerned with considerations of Development. Within the Model we identify that the element of Performance exists naturally only in the area above the Axis, while the elements of Purpose and Process only exist below the Axis.

Once again we emphasise that this is not a cosmetic or semantic difference. One of the difficulties that organisations face in handling the volume of information that is available to inform their management development thinking rests in not separating the steps of Development and Performance.

Continuing with the etching process we start to reveal that although we have identified the existence of each of the elements and that they each have the appropriate Content, for effective management development the elements need to be linked.

This is the third of our Critical Checks - the **Critical Check for Platform Connections**.

In our Model each of the five P elements is linked to every other. Furthermore, this is not just a draughting nicety to make the Model look better. The Critical Check for Connections tests the quality and the strength of each of these linkages by asking key questions.

By way of illustration, the Connection between the elements of Purpose and

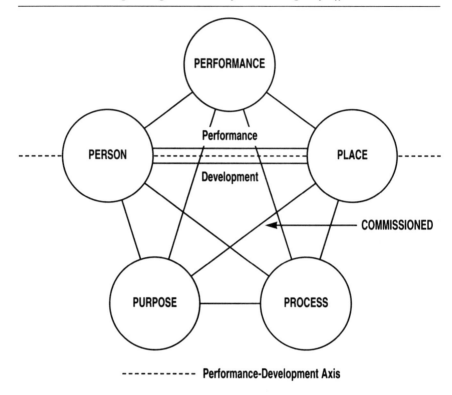

----------- **Performance-Development Axis**

Platform Connections

Place is the one that we call Commissioned. The Critical Check is looking at whether the identified development objectives carry weight in the organisation and whether they are championed with appropriate authority.

Each of the Connections has a title (a word beginning with the letter C), which encapsulates the spirit of the question that is being asked.

The 5 As

You will by now be starting to see the way that these Critical Checks take you logically and rigorously around the Wadenhoe Model.

As you work through the later chapters of the book there are a series of check lists that will help to provide the rigour and challenge to your management development thinking that we believe is a key strength of the Model.

However, at this stage in the thinking we also recognise the potential limitations of our traditional approach to management development. We have proceeded round the Model in the relatively naive view that the problems with the lack of managerial performance will be resolved through some form of management development intervention.

The role of the five **Analysis** steps that we now introduce is to test those assumptions. In each of these steps we triangulate our thinking by linking together three of the five P elements at a time.

Let us look at a specific example.

In working around the Model you will have developed your understanding of just what the elements of Performance, Person and Place look like in your organisation. The first of the Analysis steps links these three elements together and asks the question:

● **Is it possible for this Performance to be achieved by these People in this Place?**

In other words we are asking you to really think about the realities of your situation.

But what if the answer is 'No'? If you do not believe that these managers are going to achieve the performance that you require in this environment, what are you going to do about it?

At this point in developing our understanding of the Model we introduce the

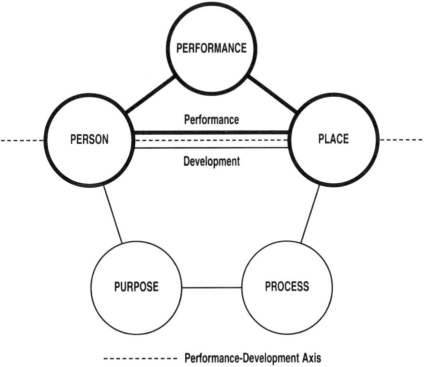

------------ **Performance-Development Axis**

Performance Potential Analysis

idea of moving outside the traditional territory of management development in order to address the issues that are being raised in the larger context of the organisation. We have called this 'going off-line'.

When we consider our answers to the questions that are being raised in this Performance Potential Analysis there are a number of steps that could be taken. If we believe that these managers are incapable of delivering the required performance irrespective of the size and scope of the management development intervention, we have to consider:

- Going off-line from Performance and perhaps rethinking the viability of the organisation's strategy, or

- Going off-line from Person and looking at aspects of our staffing and recruitment and at the potential to replace some of the current managers, or

- Going off-line from Place and looking at the facilities, resources, systems and infrastructure of the organisation that might need to be addressed.

These are key considerations that are not part of traditional management development thinking; thus the further rigour of the Model is in ensuring that we do not go forward blindly or naively with a management development initiative that is not going to provide the results that the organisation requires. It requires management development to integrate forcefully into the rest of the organisation's activities.

Up to this point the Critical Checks have been concerned with the internal consistency of the 5P Platform and the quality of the thinking that links together the elements.

Through the five Analysis steps we have introduced the third dimension of the Model, which is where it reminds us that management development is a means to a means to an end - the means to achieve management performance, which in turn is the means to achieve organisational performance. If the achievement of the managerial performance that we require means that we have to address aspects of the culture of the organisation that currently disable managerial performance, then in our thinking this is a legitimate development activity.

The five Analysis steps are covered in Chapter 7 and look at:

Performance Potential Analysis
Development Needs Analysis
Development Place Analysis
Process Design Analysis
Cost Benefit Analysis.

Making Management Development Live in the Organisation

The next of our five Critical Checks is concerned with the way that the Model is Constructed. The role of the **Critical Check for Platform Construction** is to ensure that the process of putting the Model together involving Communication, Consultation, etc, leads to an effective launch. The Critical Check is aimed at ensuring that any management development initiative is rooted in the heart of the organisation rather than being seen as 'another Personnel procedure'.

It is concerned with Checking the level of understanding and Commitment that exists in the relevant parts of the organisation for the proposed management development intervention. Have all the interested parties been consulted and do they really understand the implications of what is being proposed? This is the Critical Check to ensure that when the intervention is actually launched we have done everything possible to predicate for success.

The final of our five Critical Checks is the **Critical Check for Platform Carrying-Out**.

We see no let-up in the rate at which the competitive and technological environment is changing. Organisational life will continue to become more complex and dynamic. In turn this means that the demands we are placing on managers will also continue to change at an increasing rate.

Gone are the days when a management development programme could be expected to continue unchanged for year after year. The essence of the Carrying-Out Check is about monitoring and learning about interventions and modifying them as we go along so that they continue to meet the needs of the organisation. The last of our Checks is therefore concerned with ensuring that appropriate processes and activities are put in place for maintaining and modifying the outcomes from the Model in the light of changing circumstances.

Conclusion

We have set out in this Chapter to provide an Executive overview of the Wadenhoe Model and the way in which it works to make management development strategically effective. We have also touched on some of the detail that illustrates the rigour that application of the Model could bring to your management development thinking.

At the same time we have not provided any answers! We said at the outset that the intention of the Model was to be **Generaliseable** and **Simple** and that we would require you to provide the **Accuracy** by the way that you work through the Model and apply its thinking to your organisation.

So what do you do now?

In the rest of the book we will take you through every aspect of the Wadenhoe Model in detail and in a way that enables you to understand it better, then apply it to your organisation.

In Chapter 9 we talk about the concept of a management development 'League Table' as a way of locating the current sophistication of your management development activities and identifying how the Model can help to promote their standing in your organisation.

We are confident that the Wadenhoe Model is a powerful tool for increasing the probability that your management development efforts will bear fruit, a confidence that arises from using the Model regularly with our clients. The participants on our programme 'Making Management Development Strategically Effective' have also confirmed its practical value.

But there is still work to be done. We believe that the Model advances our thinking about management development. We hope that it will lead more organisations to see management development as an investment rather than as a cost.

To strengthen the Model still further the next phase of the research builds on this position by looking at 'Putting a Measure on Management Development', and this is the theme for Chapter 10.

Checklist for Chapter 2

These checklist items are addressed primarily at the organisation's Chief Executive:

● Are you clear about the managerial performance that your organisation's business strategy demands?

● Can you identify how your own performance contributes to the achievement of your organisation's business strategy?

● How well informed are your managers about the performance that is expected of them, and how well are they currently performing against the standards that you have set?

● Do you believe that your managers are capable of performing in the manner and to the standards that you require?

● Are you confident that management development objectives are well defined before any activities are undertaken?

● What activities and processes are used for management development in your organisation? Is there a particular method that predominates? Is there sound logic for using any particular method (as opposed to fad or personal preference)?

- Does the environment in your organisation
  enable managers to perform in the way that you require?
  encourage development particularly in experimentation and the taking of risks in the process of learning?

- How well are all the five P elements of the 5P Platform being taken into account in thinking about management development in your organisation? Are there any obvious omissions?

- Do you demand to understand the benefits that will accrue to the business from your investment in a particular management development activity?

- Do you evaluate the changes in managerial performance that have occurred as a result of your investment in management development?

- Who is held accountable for the development of managers in your organisation? To what extent is their thinking similar to that of the Wadenhoe Model?

Chapter 3
'CREATING THE TEMPLATE' - THE 5P PLATFORM

Development Objectives

By the end of this Chapter we intend that you will:

- Understand in detail the role and meaning of each of the P elements of the 5P Platform of the Wadenhoe Model

- Understand the importance of the Performance-Development Axis in addressing both managerial performance and management development

- Be able to relate each of the P elements to your own organisation

- Understand the implications of the omission of any of the five P elements from your organisation's thinking about management development

- Understand the implications of any of the five P elements being under- or over-developed or emphasised in your organisation's thinking about management development.

Experience of Management Development

The frustrations and the concerns that led to our research and to this book are described in Chapter 1. They resulted in a group of experienced management development professionals convening to pool their knowledge and experience of management development events, processes and interventions. We believed that

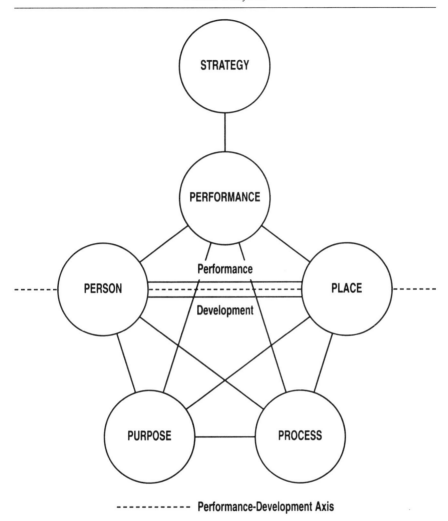

----------- **Performance-Development Axis**

this would lead to ways in which we could improve the effectiveness of management development activities.

We started by examining in detail our own experiences of management development interventions over the years. We were looking for the factors that distinguished the successful interventions from the less successful. We sought common factors across the interventions that we could objectively identify as having delivered what the client organisation required and that in some way were absent from those that we judged to have been less successful.

The process of pooling and filtering took many hours of meetings, discussion, reflection and analysis. As already stated, with our experience we knew that there would be no 'magic ingredient' that we had overlooked in the past, but even a small 'Aha!' moment would have been welcome!

It is relevant at this stage to mention that our experiences showed that we had each encountered uncertainties on the part of both individuals and the organisations in which they worked about the meaning of management development. So once again, the definition of management development to which we work is:

'A Planned and Purposeful Process for enabling managers' Performance in their Place of work.'

Although we recognised at the beginning of our research that there was a very substantial quantity and variety of data and issues that needed to be taken into account in designing and delivering effective management development interventions, we also recognised that one of the significant characteristics of the less successful interventions was an absence of the key data and insufficient attention being paid to key issues.

The sheer volume of data required and often available for the management development professional was a problem in itself and we therefore sought ways of sorting and grouping information into manageable 'sub-sets'. Eventually we managed to group the data and the issues under five main headings. These were:

● Data and issues concerned with the selection and/or development of processes appropriate for a particular management development intervention

● Data and issues concerned with the identification of the purposes of the management development intervention and the definition of the outcomes to be achieved

● Data and issues related to the population of managers whose development is being targeted. Description of the characteristics and status of the individuals in relation to both their managerial performance and further development needs

● Data and issues concerned with the organisational context - its culture, environmental features and infrastructure. Illumination of factors helpful and hindering to managers' development and performance achievement

● Data and issues concerning the performances required of managers. Identification of the key contributions demanded of managers by their organisations.

These broad headings will not surprise anyone actively involved in management development, whether as a specialist or line manager. Essentially they are derived from the common-sense world of a 'need to know', and address the why, what, where, who and how of any initiatives we undertake. The groupings serve as an easy means of identifying our information needs, organising the data collection, sorting information and clarifying issues for subsequent processing, decision-making and action planning.

Such a treatment lays the foundation for the development of a framework for informing the design and delivery of management development initiatives. We have called the resulting framework the Wadenhoe Model.

The further development of the Model went beyond the screening and analysis of our own experience of management development work, and tapped into and extracted from the experience of other practitioners in the field. Thus we researched the literature on management development; we spoke to our contacts (both peers and clients); we took every opportunity both to talk about and to test out our emerging framework with management development and line managers; and, as we grew in confidence, we also started to use the framework to inform our own practice.

What has emerged is a model that works, a model that provides management developers with an organiser for their thinking and decision-making as they seek to construct and implement an effective management development strategy for their organisations.

The Foundations of The Wadenhoe Model

The five groupings depicted in the previous section provide the elements of the Wadenhoe Model, and comprise the **5P Platform**, the description of which forms the substance for much of the remainder of this Chapter. The 5P Platform is located on an Axis, which enables the Model to be used to address both managerial Performance and managerial Development, a crucial feature of the Model in ensuring the effectiveness and impact of management development initiatives. This **Performance-Development Axis** will also be discussed later in this Chapter.

The five elements of the Platform are linked together by 'cross-bracing', or Connections. These Connections serve to integrate the various Platform elements into a cohesive and resilient whole. The Connections will be discussed in Chapter 6.

The elements of the **5P Platform** and their Connections provide the focus for a number of **Critical Checks**, which provide for the critical assessment of the developing Wadenhoe Model. We have identified five categories of Critical Checks, covering the Completeness of the Model, its Content, its Connections, its Construction, and the Carrying-Out of its application in continued use. Each of these Critical Checks will be examined in detail in the next Chapter.

In use the Wadenhoe Model is demanding, calling for intelligent data-gathering, organising, processing and critiquing. Its strength is in its discipline and rigour and in prompting us to make our assumptions explicit. In working through its various facets there is, however, the danger - perversely so for a Model that focuses attention, aids clarity, and seeks wholeness - that the user can get side-tracked and bogged down, and lose sight of the wood for the trees. To prevent this we have developed a recommended further process of **Analysis** involving five steps. Following these steps should ensure that the user of the Model maintains a critical stance without reaching paralysis by analysis; maintains a focus on key issues without developing tunnel vision; and makes encouraging and demonstrable progress in eating the whole elephant - but one piece at a time. The analyses also serve to place a boundary around those issues that are 'on-line', that is within the territory of management development, while at the same time alerting us to other aspects and actions that require to be addressed and prosecuted 'off-line' (for example, selection and de-selection rather than development of managers; job restructuring rather than manager development; systems rather than skills development, etc). The five-step **Analysis** will be fully explored in Chapter 7.

The 5P Platform

From the review of our experiences of what distinguished effective management development initiatives from the less successful, we sorted the information that emerged into the five broad groups identified above. These groupings were then further refined and ultimately became the five elements, or 'Ps', in the 5P Platform of the Wadenhoe Model.

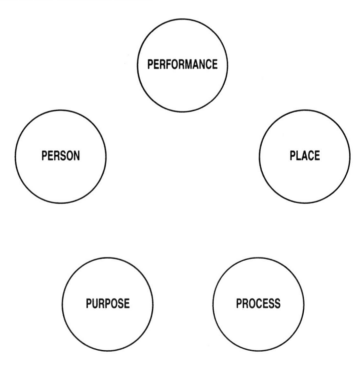

Giving each element of the Model a single-word title starting with the same initial letter is clearly for impact and for easier recall, but these title words have specific meanings within the Model, and it is important that their meanings are understood in the way that we are using them.

The rest of this Chapter describes each of the elements in sufficient detail to enable you to look at your own organisation and determine whether these elements are given sufficient consideration in your management development thinking. We will return to the content of each of these elements in Chapter 5 when we consider how to carry out the Critical Checks on the quality and the necessity of the information required.

Element 1 - Performance

We found that for Performance to be defined in terms that are useful it is necessary to break it up into the areas of activity in which managers are required to perform. We call these areas the Competence Domains. The Model requires that the domains be identified both in terms of what is currently demanded of managers, and what will be demanded of them in the foreseen future. Examples of Competence Domains are given in Appendix 2.

When we are considering managerial roles in our organisations, whether for recruitment, restructuring, appraisal, promotion, reward or placement, how often do we clearly identify and define the Performance required of managers?

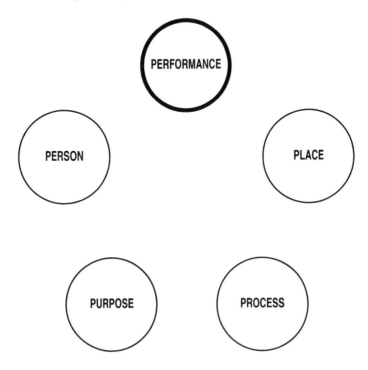

The continuing growth in performance-related bonus and pay schemes has certainly focused attention on measurable output targets such as sales volume, profits and warranty claims. But from our research we know there is still a reluctance or an inability for organisations to specify the performance areas required to be addressed by managers in order to achieve such outputs.

The language of management is changing and we now see competence, performance and contribution domains all in use. The rolling bandwagon of the competency movement, the birth of the Management Charter Initiative, and the rise of vocational training have all added additional and related terminology such as performance standards and elements, etc, as well as bringing further impetus to the drive to illuminate and define managerial performance requirements.

However, any framework sets out to be Generaliseable, Simple and Accurate, and struggles with the conflict that only two of these three desirable attributes are achievable at any one time. Like the Wadenhoe Model, many competence frameworks aim to be Generaliseable and Simple and rely on the individual organisation to supply the Accuracy by interpreting the framework in the context of their situation. Unfortunately, we observe that many of the exercises instigated by organisations to define Performance are built solely on the generalisations, and do not take sufficient account of the real strategic needs of the specific organisation.

As a result the outcomes of the exercise can be bland and meaningless, and have often been shrugged off by managers as 'another Personnel exercise'. For personnel people as well, they provide an inadequate starting point for targeted management development and often become little more than a ritual that has no real relevance to or bearing on the subsequent design and content of development activities.

Snapshot

We often find Leadership appearing - quite correctly - as one of the Competence Domains for many managers. But what precisely do we mean by Leadership in the context of a particular role in our organisation: is it the technical leadership that is required by a head of function; the living leadership of the organisation's values and beliefs; the charismatic leadership of new ventures; or something completely different? If the concept of Competence Domains is to be a useful one there clearly needs to be more precision in their specification.

Without a clear understanding of the Performance that we require of an individual or group of managers it is very hard to see how to start to assess their development needs in any meaningful way.

Furthermore, we need to be in a position to define not only the Competence Domains for the role now but also to be able to anticipate the demands that the future strategy of the organisation will place on the role.

By rigorously defining the Performance that we require of each managerial role in our organisation we have the basis for determining and evaluating the current performance of each job holder against the Performance required for that role. This in turn provides us with objective information on the gaps that exist between the Present State of managerial Performance and the Desired State, and therefore starts to focus our thinking about appropriate management development.

So within this element of Performance we are looking for a clear definition of the Competence Domains for each managerial role in the organisation. In addition, to move our management development thinking forward, we are also looking for some objective appraisal of the current performance of individuals against the Domains and the standards that are required of the role.

Element 2 - Person

The element of Person in the Model relates to the individual's Competencies and Characteristics that are required in order to be able to perform effectively in the Competence Domains. Having identified the Competence Domains that are required of each role or position in the organisation and the criteria for success in each of these,

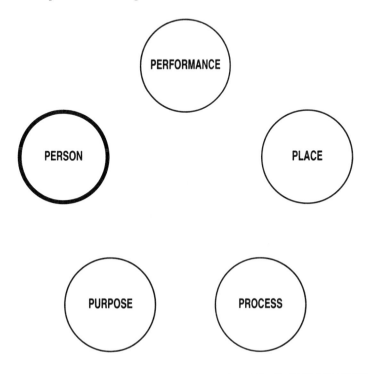

we are now able to define the Competencies and Characteristics that are necessary for an individual to perform in that Domain and to the desired standards.

Competencies and Characteristics for the purpose of the Model are the behaviours, knowledge, skills, attitudes and personal attributes that are required of managers in order to perform in the required way and to the required standards. This element takes into account the Present State of the individual as well as the future Desired State.

Management development initiatives often make assumptions about individual managers and their need for development. Sometimes they are not considered as individuals at all. A not untypical scenario is for a programme to be devised and run with subsequent surprise when some participants say that is was not relevant for them. The element of Person in the Wadenhoe Model aims to focus the thinking on your organisation's managers rather than on an idealised and fictitious individual.

Snapshot

Having worked on a Team Leaders programme for one part of a major distribution organisation, we were asked by another part of the same company to 'give the same course for our people'. They strongly resisted our request to meet their people so that the development programme could be tailored to meet their needs. Their thinking failed initially to acknowledge the cultural, ethnic, age and experience differences that would have made a straight copy of the original programme inappropriate.

We have found that this analysis is not always carried out with sufficient thoroughness. Equally, we have observed a tendency to leap quickly from symptom to solution without taking sufficient account of the actual managers involved, their typical patterns of behaviour and their characteristics.

However, with an accurate and objective analysis of the Competencies and Characteristics that are required, organisations are able to carry out the second critical stage of the assessment. This requires identification of those particular areas of knowledge, skills and attitudes in which the individual is deficient. Only with this quality of individual knowledge are we able to specify where development is needed to achieve the required Performance.

This level of analysis ensures that any development activity is very sharply focused and therefore has a better chance of being effective.

The Performance-Development Axis

Rotation of the 5P Platform on its Performance-Development Axis prompts us to consider Person not only in terms of Competencies and Characteristics relating to ability to perform in the managerial role, but also as a participant in development activities and processes. We therefore need also to understand and specify in detail the Competencies and Characteristics necessary for the individual to *develop*.

Snapshot

An engineering company initiated a development programme for a particular level of managers, all of whom were said to have potential for wider responsibilities. Among those selected for the programme were two managers who from the outset showed limited ability to comprehend the programme's content. Follow-up visits showed that they also could not understand the application of the ideas to their jobs. It was also clear that both were struggling with the demands of their current jobs. One was significantly failing to handle a part of the process that was ailing. It is very doubtful that either could succeed in management roles in the way that the company required, however much they were exposed to development activities. The Peter Principle in action?

It has been recognised for some time by management development specialists (though hardly acknowledged by our general education system!) that individuals

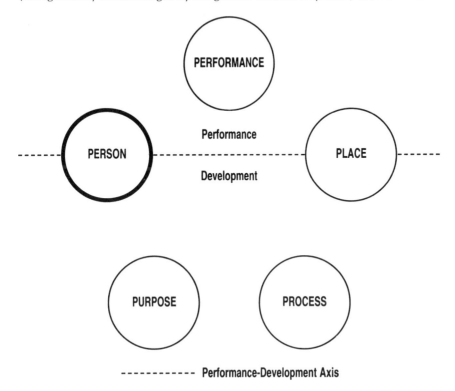

have their own preferred ways of learning. Just as it may be futile for a manager who is innumerate to attend a 'Finance for Non-Financial Managers' course, so it may also be ineffective for a manager who is unable or unwilling to learn from experience to take part in an outdoor development programme.

Element 3 - Purpose

The element of Purpose is concerned with identifying and making explicit the outcomes required of a development activity or process. Purpose will comprise the aims, goals and objectives for development, and as such will provide the essential frame for designing, implementing and evaluating the initiative.

Snapshot

Re-organisation within an oil company changed the role of its engineering department from being an engineering service to becoming an internal consultancy for the whole company. This was a radical and, for some, bewildering change affecting the several hundred members of this department. As part of the supporting development of its managers a series of one-week programmes was commissioned. The objectives for this programme were that the participants should be able to do the following:

● understand the role of the internal consultant and to recognise and begin to develop the skills required to make this role effective

● identify any personal barriers to carrying out this role and develop a personal plan for overcoming these

● be able to recognise the reactions to major change that they will be likely to meet and to understand the implications of these for the management of their staff, and

● understand the issues likely to affect their staff's thinking about career development and how this will affect their motivation

These intentions were well understood and processes were designed that the managers accepted and found effective. It was in the financial area that difficulty was encountered. It proved hard to define the performance required of managers in this area and clear objectives were not really agreed. On each run of the course participants were dissatisfied - not with the tutorial competence but with the perceived lack of relevance of the finance sessions.

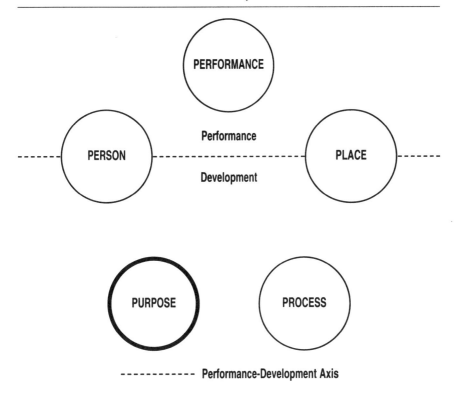

------------ Performance-Development Axis

The effective management of people and performance requires that we are able to set and monitor relevant, well-defined objectives. So it should be with management development. Without a clear statement of the development objectives that is shared and agreed between line managers, participants and provider, it is hard to see how the full potential of the management development investment can be realised.

In saying this, we recognise that the slavish setting of objectives from the start can restrict the potency of some of the more open-ended learning processes, such as action learning. However, we are familiar with programmes of this genre that have foundered through lack of vision of the possibilities for learning outcomes. The more effective learning seems to be related to the ability of the participant in such a process to be able to define what he or she has to achieve in learning terms, as well as project terms at some time within the programme, though not necessarily at the outset.

Element 4 - Process
We use the term Process to encompass both the methods and the content of a particular development initiative. It is not uncommon for discussions between clients and providers of management development initiatives to focus on content rather than process and appear to be driven by the inputs required.

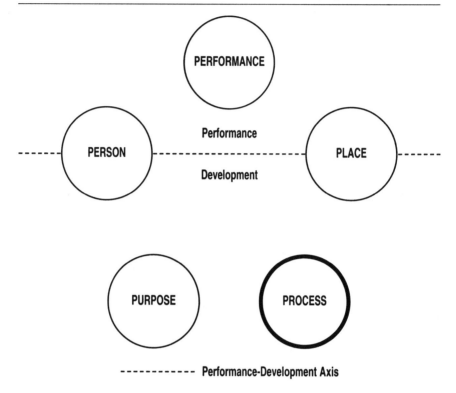

----------- **Performance-Development Axis**

In focusing on the element of Process in the 5P Platform, we are therefore concerned to highlight not only the necessary content but also appropriate learning processes. The identification and planning of development activities needs to be based on an awareness of the vast range of available learning methods - Andrej Huczinski's *Encyclopedia of Learning Methods* lists over 300!

Beyond choice of method, the design of the processes of development needs to be based in sound learning principles. *Learning* is the core process of management development, not - and unfortunately this is all too often the case - *training*.

Effective learning design demands a thorough understanding of learning theory and its applications. Such an understanding re-emphasises the great variety of possible learning process and, in so doing, discredits the all too often 'one best way' promulgated by advocates of particular and favoured methods and approaches.

It is not our intention to exclude or decry any particular development process or to propose our own favoured solutions. One strength of the Wadenhoe Model is that it requires consideration of the alternatives that are available and then to select the most appropriate for the development that is desired.

Element 5 - Place

The element of Place is concerned with the physical and the cultural environment in which both the development and the managerial performance must be delivered. In other words, this is the context in which people perform and develop. For some development processes (coaching, mentoring, understudying, and some forms of action learning, for example) it is one and the same Place.

It is our assertion that the only place in which managerial performance matters is the manager's real world of his or her work. We also assert that the extent to which concepts are grasped during any development activity is irrelevant if

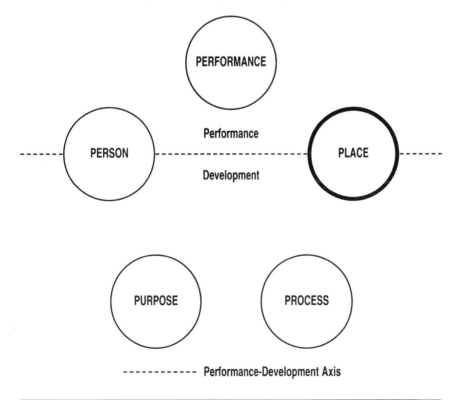

these concepts do not translate into improved performance at work. That is not to put a time constraint on the results and to say that there must be visible improvement immediately the individual returns to work. While gaining new ideas and insights is likely to have an effect on individual personal development, it is certainly in terms of improved performance that the organisation expects to see a return on its management development investment.

In using the Wadenhoe Model we are concerned therefore with changes in managerial performance at work not just with the absorption of concepts at some off-the-job venue.

We have seen that sometimes the gap in managerial performance will not be bridged by conventional management development activities. The blockages may well not be located in the Competencies and Characteristics of the managers. The motivational climate within the organisation can actively discourage the individual from performing in the desired way and to the desired standard.

Snapshot

First-line supervisors in a manufacturing company were commenting on factors affecting their supervisory performance. They emphasised:

- The performance-related pay system - the 'package' was considered to be 'all right', but its application was poor, not reflecting the merit of those in the lower positions, chiefly through not reflecting the excessive and unsociable hours they worked - there was a feeling of inequity

- Meetings - too many and little resulting from them. They only increased the already heavy time pressures on the supervisors

- Poor equipment - some described having to 'beg' for adequate equipment for the job to be done

- Ten-hour shifts in which there were no breaks

- Lack of senior management response to their suggestions

They commented on their perception of senior management's view of motivation - five-a-side football, netball, social club, bowling and snooker. 'When someone's been at work since 6.00 am they don't want to stay on for these. They're shattered. In any case they don't really affect your will to work harder or better.'

So before we engage in any development activities, whether formal or informal, we need to review whether the physical environment, the organisational structures and systems necessary to mobilise the desired Performance are in place. Do the organisation's culture and climate, conventions and customs actively support and encourage the desired managerial performance? This is more than just a 'nice to have' or a 'feel good factor'. We have at times encountered the naive belief that managerial performance can be changed by a course and transferred directly to the workplace with no other intervention.

Snapshot

A manufacturing company arranged a modular development programme for senior managers. The programme enthused most of them to try different ways of doing things and also caused some of them to question the most senior management about strategic matters. The aggressive response from the Managing Director and other senior management put the whole of the programme at peril and the participants were left wondering whether changing the way they did things was worthwhile.

The Performance-Development Axis

When we looked at the element of Person earlier in the Chapter we identified the existence of an Axis that runs across the 5P Platform. This Axis recognises that we need to consider aspects of the individual managers that affect their ability and willingness to perform separately from the factors that affect their ability and willingness to develop. The same is also true of the element of Place.

We have focused earlier on features of the work environment that will impact on individuals' motivation to perform as the organisation requires. Equally we need to look at the features of the environment that are likely to affect individuals' willingness to experiment and learn. We have long recognised that the nature of the venue for an off-the-job learning event is a design consideration. But more importantly we are concerned here with the environment at work and the impact that this will have on development.

If we acknowledge and accept that Performance at work is the focus of development, it follows that some change and therefore some experimentation will need to take place at work as individuals try to affect their managerial performance. The element of Place below the Performance-Development Axis is concerned with these issues.

Increasingly organisations are acknowledging the importance of learning in ensuring survival and beyond that providing a competitive edge in these increasingly turbulent times. Total quality and continuous improvement, for example, demand widespread and on-going learning by the organisation's members - not least its managers!

Similarly, the notion of 'learning organisations' where learning is recognised as a key ingredient in organisational success is built upon the premise of learning being a continuous process and a natural process. Unfortunately there is also recognition that the natural process of learning may be limited, haphazard, blocked and insufficient within the culture of our organisations. We see organisations increasingly stimulating their employees towards any type of learning merely to improve their receptivity to the real learning that the organisation requires.

These then are the issues that are being considered within Place below the Performance-Development Axis.

Snapshot

On the surface it might be hard to see how an evening class in a subject unrelated to business can improve managerial performance. However, one of the organisations that we talked to showed how an evening class in Drama for an individual with a speech problem led to more confidence and increased performance at work.

Performance, Person, Purpose, Process and **Place** - these then are the five Ps constituting our Platform for effective management development.

'Why, who, what, how and where? - we know that,' you might be saying. 'So what?'

Our research group said exactly the same when we first looked at what was emerging from our discussions. Knowing that these elements are important we asked ourselves these supplementary questions:

- 'Are they the most important elements?'

- 'Have we always taken them into account with the required thoroughness?'

From our own experience we concluded that these were indeed the most important factors, but that to be practically useful we needed to be clearer about what was essential within each element.

The answer we gave to the second question was embarrassing. We had to admit that we have not always taken all the elements into account. The amount of information available is often daunting and the interactions between the elements provide further complications. Furthermore, we recognised that in some organisations the required information was not readily available. Or maybe it was available but the issues were of such political sensitivity that leaving them 'for the time being' seemed the most expedient course of action.

In other words, a particular P was missing or under-represented in our thinking and decision-making. This is an issue that we will explore in more detail in the next Chapter dealing with 'skews' and 'omissions'.

The real issue was our ability to organise the information that we had in a way that enabled us to make decisions that would increase the effectiveness of what we did.

In the next Chapter we will look at each of these elements more critically to start to put some order on the information that we have accumulated.

Entry Points to The Model

Having identified what we believed were the key factors that needed to be addressed in making decisions about management development in organisations, we then returned to our own experience to look at the way that various clients had typically approached these factors.

It became clear to us that there were a range of possible starting points in considering the five Ps, and we identified examples of each entry point to the 5P Platform.

Some management development initiatives are first conceived with a specific process in mind - 'I want a course using the outdoors'. Others start with specific content - 'We need the latest stuff in marketing'. Still other initiatives have their origins in accreditation requirements, or a culture shift. While none of these approaches is necessarily wrong, the starting points have strong implications. The strength of the Model is to make the thinking behind these initiatives explicit.

To understand the implications of these different starting points, let us consider each of the elements of the 5P Platform.

Development event or Initiative that is Person-led
Where management development initiatives are grounded foremost in the consideration of the Person

Here the concern is to develop the people in the organisation almost as an end in itself. Education, personal development and the fulfilment of individual potential are often valued for their own sake, though this stance may also be underpinned by a belief in the importance of the human asset to the competitiveness of the organisation. In this latter sense management development may be regarded as an investment for the future. Additionally, the provision of individual development opportunities may form part of a recruitment package, or a reward, or a retention scheme. Whatever, the entry point into the 5P Platform is Person-led.

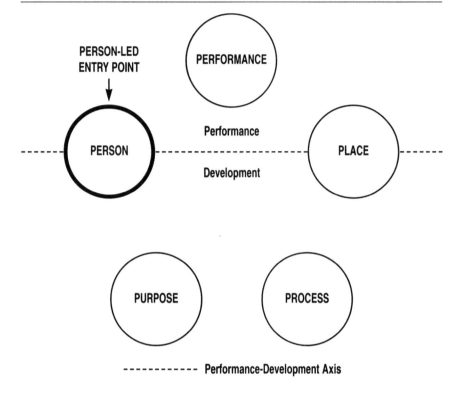

- - - - - - - - - - - **Performance-Development Axis**

Development event or Initiative that is Purpose-led

Consideration is given first to the Development Objectives

Such an objective is often externally generated by the stipulations and requirements of professional membership criteria, national curricula for various forms of
qualifications and certification. Also, Purpose-led development may arise from
new legislative demands, for example on health and safety in the workplace.

Development event or Initiative that is Process-led

Where an organisation is riding on a particular development bandwagon

Here the entry point into the 5P Platform is via a favoured development process. The
Favoured Process - and not unusually the bandwagon - might be action learning, computer-based learning, self-development, outdoor development, or others. The issue
again is not that any of these processes will not be developmental, but rather that a
process has been selected irrespective of whether it is appropriate for the nature of
learning that is actually required. The implication is that there is a single ideal development process for the managers of that organisation, which, of course, might be true.
However, the Wadenhoe Model requires that this assumption be tested and confirmed.

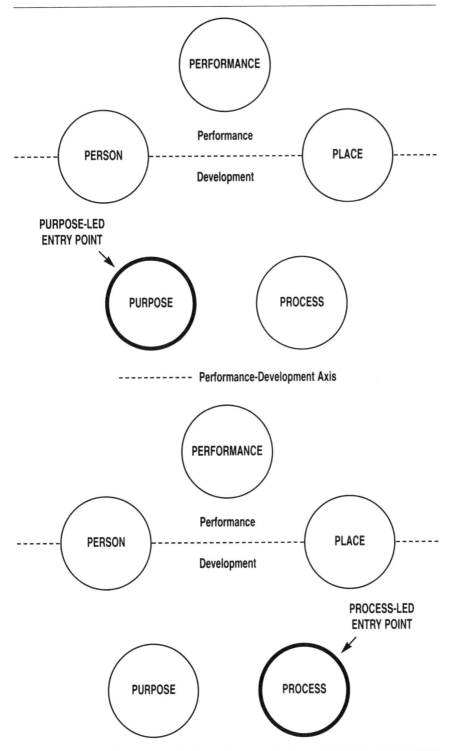

Development event or Initiative that is Place-led
Where the culture and other issues of the environment of the organisation have determined the starting point

Many of the management development initiatives we identified as being led by Place went beyond instrumentality to being based in ideological beliefs in 'how we should now do things around here'. Thus shifts towards self-directed work teams, empowerment, networking, de-layering and so on may become not just means to an end but ends in themselves. Again, we are not trying to gainsay any of these organisation development activities, but we question the completeness of the thinking where management development initiatives are led by this entry point alone.

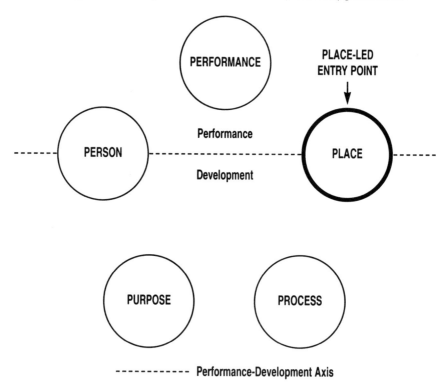

---------- Performance-Development Axis

Development event or Initiative that is Performance-led - the Strategic Hook
Management development should be a key strategic tool. This leads us to believe that the Hook into management development must be the link between the declared strategy of the organisation and the Performance that this demands of managers. This is not to say that our understanding of corporate strategy does not also inform our decisions about the culture and systems of the organisation (Place) and the type of people that we need to deliver the strategy (Person).

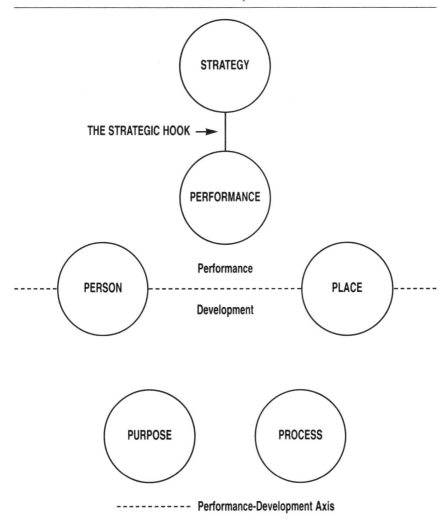

Performance-Development Axis

However, we have seen that the link most often absent from any organisation's strategic thinking is the managerial performance that is required to achieve the organisation's strategic ambitions. This means defining with some considerable clarity the behaviours required of managers.

For the remainder of the book we shall assume a Strategic Hook for the Model. For this to be a reality we must be able to understand the strategy where it is made explicit or to imply a strategy where it is not. Without understanding the strategic aspirations of the organisation the basic thrust of this book, 'Making Management Development Strategically Effective', fails. Without understanding the strategy nothing can be strategically effective except by accident. The challenge for HR professionals is drawing from the declared strategy the implications for managers and articulating these in a way that is both coherent and acceptable.

Snapshot

Working with the HR Director of a major PLC on aspects of his HR strategy required two days of challenging, questioning and discussion before he was able to clarify the managerial implications of the company's business strategy, which was largely held in the Chairman's head. Only then were we able to start to look at the required performance of the Directors and senior managers if they were to turn the strategy into reality.

Summary

So far we have looked at the nature of the 5P Platform of the Wadenhoe Model and the points at which different organisations have entered the Model for their approaches to management development.

The purpose of the 5P Platform is to provide a framework for organising the volume of data that we believe needs to be considered in making our management development decisions. Having effectively sorted this information into these groups, the obvious question is 'What do we do with it now?'.

The next Chapter looks at the concept of the Critical Checks that must be made to be able to look at the extent to which the data that we have is complete - whether we have addressed the key issues within each of the Ps. These key issues are those that experience tells up predicate for success or failure in management development initiatives. Beyond each individual P, the Critical Checks focus our attention on the interactions and necessary interconnections that must be considered and put in place if our initiatives are to comprise of compatible, mutually supporting and self-reinforcing components so that our plans do not literally fall apart on implementation.

Checklist for Chapter 3

● Are you able to define each of the P elements clearly for your organisation, and the nature of the content of each of them?

● Are you able to distinguish between Competence Domains, Criteria and Competencies? (These are the terms we use, but different terms may well be in use for the same concepts.)

● Is there a definition of the Competence Domains for each of the roles that you are considering for development? Who is responsible for defining these? To what extent is responsibility accepted for doing this? How well are the principles for defining performance understood?

- When you consider the individual manager for development do you compare the Competencies they currently possess with those required for Performance in the defined Domains?

- Does the method of appraisal in your organisation, whether formal or informal, produce the quality of information about individuals that you require for sound management development actions?

- Does your organisation consider the managers as individuals or are they somehow lumped together for development purposes?

- Before you start any management development activity are the development objectives clearly defined and recorded?

- Do you consider a range of alternative development methods before making a decision as to which would be the most appropriate? Do you have the capability to ask the right questions about development processes of an external supplier, eg consultants, business school?

- Do your organisation's culture, climate, conventions, customs, systems and procedures actively support and encourage the desired management performance and development?

- When you start thinking about management development in your organisation, where does your thinking start? With Person, Purpose, Process, Place or through the Strategic Hook into Performance?

- Do you understand the business aspirations for your organisation and their implications for management and management development?

Chapter 4
'STACKING THE ODDS FOR SUCCESS' - THE CRITICAL CHECKS

Introduction

This Chapter takes the Model a stage further through describing the nature of the Critical Checks that need to be made to test the emphasis, completeness, rigour, strength and appropriateness of the Wadenhoe Model in its assembly, development and application. The purpose of the Checks is to stack the odds that, in use, the Model delivers both strategic and effective management development.

We had recognised that the basic 5P Platform was a useful start but was insufficient for our intentions of providing a framework for thinking and action in planning, designing and delivering management development initiatives. More exploration was required. Verification checks needed to be made to test that the usage of the Model was as robust as it should be. We shall refer to these in future as the 'Critical Checks'.

Five Critical Checks

As we described in the previous Chapter, the assembly of the 5P Platform requires considerable information. Within the research team we needed to know whether we could identify the information that was absolutely vital and critical from within the information available. This led us to establishing five Critical Checks that needed to be carried out to ensure that we were looking at the right decisions to make our management development activities strategically effective.

We identified that we needed to verify that:

1 the 5P Platform was in fact complete

2 the critical ingredients of each of the elements of the Platform had been identified

3 the elements of the 5P Platform had been systematically linked together into
a whole, and the 'cross-bracing' and connections of the Model were in place

4 the process of identifying and assembling the Model had been carried out in
a manner that predicated for a successful launch of the management development initiatives, and

5 the necessary activities were in place for maintaining and modifying the
Model in implementation and use.

In this Chapter we shall introduce each of the Critical Checks, considering in
particular the Check for Platform Completeness, since this is so fundamental to
the Model. In subsequent Chapters the other Critical Checks will be explained
in detail.

Critical Checks of The Wadenhoe Model - the 5 Cs

As an aid to recalling the elements that form the basic Platform of the Model we
used words beginning with the letter 'P' as titles for them - Performance, Person,
Purpose, Process and Place. This pattern has been followed for the Critical
Checks, which we identify as the 5 Cs - **Completeness, Content, Connection,
Construction** and **Carrying-Out**.

We admit that the last of these Cs is a little forced; the Carrying-Out Check is
concerned with critical issues concerning the implementation of the Platform as
live management development initiatives in the organisation. If you can think of
a better C word than 'Carrying-Out' we will be pleased to hear from you!

Platform Completeness Check

The focus of each of the elements of the 5P Platform (ie Performance, Person,
Purpose, Process and Place) appears both obvious and logical - almost self-evident. Yet our research identified that in some organisations one or more of the Ps
was absent from their thinking about management development.

The first of the five Critical Checks therefore looks at whether the 5P
Platform is Complete. Are all the elements taken into consideration and, if they
are, are they given equal weighting or are some elements considered to be more

important than others? These are the issues that we shall examine as we Check for Platform Completeness.

Platform Content Check

We identified earlier the wealth of information that is available in each of the P elements. But is it the right information? The Check for Content is asking whether the critical ingredients of each of the Ps have been clearly identified and considered.

Platform Connection Check

Thus far we have considered each of the elements of the 5P Platform in isolation. In seeking to avoid a fragmented approach to management development it is essential that all five Ps are interconnected. The Model needs to be cross-braced in order to create a resilient structure in which each element is compatible with and reinforcing the others. The purpose of the Connection Check is to ensure that such interconnections and linkages have been considered and built into the Model.

Platform Construction Check

This Check ensures that the specification and development of the Model is done in such a way as to demonstrate visibly a concern for the key stakeholders in the planned management development. Further, our intention is to ensure that there is a full understanding of, and commitment to, the initiative prior to its launch.

Platform Carrying-Out Check

The Wadenhoe Model is a dynamic tool to inform your management development thinking on an on-going basis and is not a static, one-off exercise. The aim of the Carrying-Out Check is to examine whether the necessary activities have been put in place for maintaining and modifying the Model during its implementation. It is essential therefore that we understand how the information within the Model will be continuously updated and modified to reflect constantly the developing strategic demands of the organisation.

These brief descriptions of the 5 Cs (or Critical Checks) of the Wadenhoe Model obviously require considerable fleshing out before they are fully fit to be of practical working value. Let us start by further examining the nature of the Platform Completeness Check.

The Platform Completeness Check

In Chapter 3 we identified that it is possible to enter the Model at very different points, and we discussed the implications of entering through any particular element. We have also found that there are different implications when one or more of the P elements is actually missing from our thinking, or, if not completely missing, so dominant (sometimes to the point of obsession) that the whole framework of the Platform is skewed in a way that severely prejudices the effectiveness of possible management development interventions.

Before turning our minds to the detail of this particular check, we should recall that the Person and Place elements of the Platform divide on an Axis, reflecting the Performance focus and the Development focus that is a critical part of the Wadenhoe Model. Above the Axis we are considering the organisational and managerial Performance issues, while below the line we are looking at issues involved in Development.

Another consideration for making our management development initiatives *strategically* effective is that there must be a link between the strategy of the organisation and the Performance required of its managers. Therefore we show the Model with a Hook between the P of Performance and the Business Strategy of the organisation. It is, in fact, on this Hook that the whole Model hangs.

In the last part of this Chapter we shall look at the implications of omissions from the Model and the distortions, biases or skews in the relative strengths of the elements this can bring.

Platform Completeness Check 1 - Performance Axis only

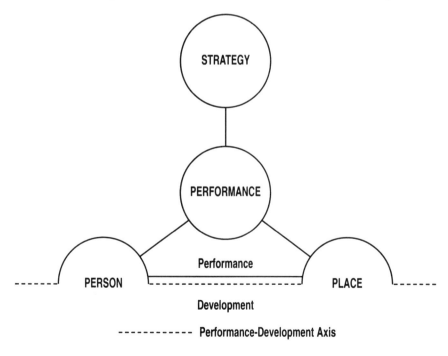

We have encountered organisations where the P elements of Performance, Person and Place exist above our Development-Performance Axis, but with nothing below the Axis to maintain the balance; such organisations have an orientation towards Performance rather than Development. The culture in these organisations is often fiercely bottom-line-driven, but the organisation provides no developmental help or facilities to enable performance to be achieved or improved. There is an expectation that individuals will drive and achieve their own development if they wish to continue to perform in the organisation.

There may be an image of 'hire and fire' within these organisations. People who do not perform tend to be replaced, as there is no framework for improving performance through development.

Snapshots

1

The newly appointed Chief Executive of a financial services company did not take long to close down the management development activities. He made known his view that in the past managers had worked to objectives that were too loosely defined and that in any case performance against these had not been well enough monitored. Toughening these processes rather than using training was going to be his approach. In future, the objective-setting process would be strengthened, as would the monitoring of performance. He also made it known that there were capable managers on the open market, and managers who did not meet the standards he required could easily be replaced.

2

The South of England manufacturing plant of a major multinational had replaced the Plant Manager four times in three years. In each case the appointment was an internal promotion of someone with a known track record. However, if they did not perform very quickly in the new role they were fired!

Platform Completeness Check 1 - Development Axis only

An alternative and surprisingly common omission is to find a Platform where the elements of Person, Purpose, Process and Place exist only below the Performance-Development Axis; the part of the Platform above the Axis is missing. Here we have development for its own sake with no sense of the value to the organisation of carrying out focused or structured development. The belief seems to exist in these organisations that the benefit will materialise in some longer-term pay-off for their investment.

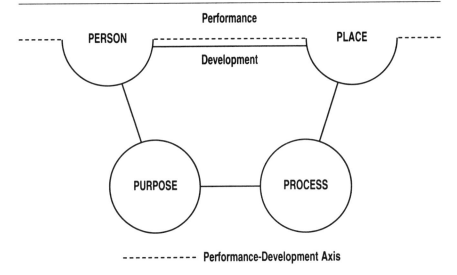

-------- Performance-Development Axis

In some organisations the responsibility for achieving benefits from the development seems to be passed to the individual with the expectations that they will draw their own sense of benefit from the development in a way that will help the organisation. Some attempts to create a learning organisation have ended up with an abdication of responsibility in this way; the organisation is relying on individuals to identify their future Performance needs and, using the available development initiatives, to equip themselves selectively for future performance.

Snapshot

The main thrust of management development in the company was to 'send' managers on a three-week residential management course at a prestigious business school. The manager responsible for management development held the view that attending the course was developmental in itself. He reported seeing changes in behaviour at work from those who attended this course, but when pressed he could not say whether these changes actually improved their managerial performance, or indeed if these development activities contributed to the company being in a better position to meet its strategic intentions.

Most managers who attended the course were enthusiastic about it but reported outcomes that were only in terms of their own personal development. None reported improved performance in their current managerial posts as an outcome.

Platform Completeness Check 2 - No Strategy

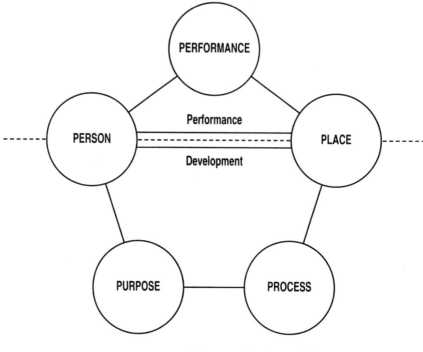

---------- **Performance-Development Axis**

Here the business Strategy is not apparent in informing the 5P Platform. It may be that the Strategy is undefined, or undeclared, or that no successful attempt has been made to explicitly translate strategic ambitions into statements of required managerial performances. The development activities may be of high quality, but are likely to be geared to making good deficiencies in current performance only.

Snapshot

A senior manager in a major insurance company had just completed a multi-million-pound project with great success. The Chief Executive invited him to 'take yourself off to Harvard or INSEAD - do a general management course - make yourself a more rounded manager'. The manager asked the obvious question: 'But what is my next job going to be? Am I going to lead another large project or become a general manager in the UK or a functional head overseas?' The CEO was unable to answer.

Platform Completeness Check 3 - No Performance

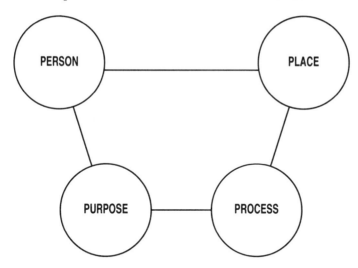

A further possible (and in our experience surprisingly frequent) omission from the 5P Platform is the element of Performance. In these organisations, while the performance and development areas are both present, the focus for improvement and development is upon Person and/or Place. In neither instance has thinking embraced the need for the clear identification of key performance areas. For example, the approach taken by the organisation may be driven by the perceived need and logic of developing personal Competencies.

Though laudable in its own right, the weakness of such an approach lies in the lack of thinking about, and follow through into, the deployment and application of these Competencies in required Performance. Thus what may emerge in the management development plan are, for example, workshops on delegation skills attended by individual contributors with no subordinates. We might also see courses on strategic thinking for operational supervisors. Each of these may be praiseworthy perhaps as providing educational opportunities, but they are difficult to justify to the line manager who is looking for a demonstrated return on this investment in terms of enhanced performance and output.

Similarly, the omission of Performance from the Platform can result in inappropriate and often costly attempts to restructure Place, ie the work environment, towards the latest thinking of a (usually American) guru, without consideration being given to just what Performance areas will be enhanced by such a shift.

Platform Completeness Check 4 - No Person

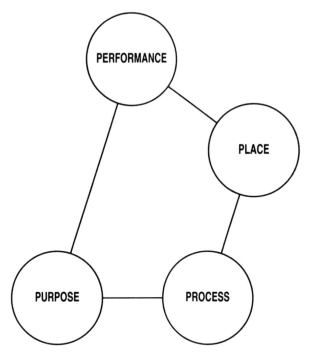

In this scenario personal Competencies and Characteristics are not identified, or differences between people acknowledged. There are two possible driving forces within these organisations. They may be driven by a definition of Competence Domains and are therefore putting all managers at a certain level through the same development process with the same development objectives irrespective of the current capabilities of the individual - an often expensive, and not necessarily effective, approach.

The second possibility is that the organisation has historically developed a training event (for example, a course) that they maintain irrespective of need. Often the key purpose of the event has long passed, but everyone who is promoted with a certain position has to attend as part of the 'rites of passage'.

In either of these circumstances cost is unlikely to be an issue and the ownership of the approach is likely to be in the senior ranks of the organisation. Attendance is not considered to be optional!

Platform Completeness Check 5 - No Purpose

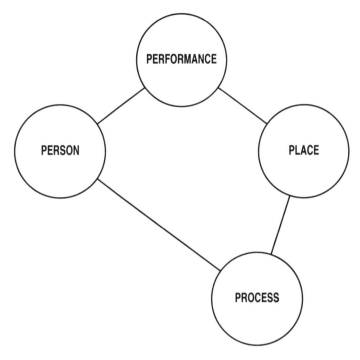

Omission of Purpose from the 5P Platform arises from a lack of identification of objectives for the management development approaches. The impact of this is often the development and delivery of open-ended but potentially aimless or unfocused initiatives. Alternatively, and often by default, it may be left to the individual managers participating in the development activities to find, make and take something of relevance or value from their involvement.

The lack of formalised development objectives also works against the establishment of objective criteria for evaluation purposes. Where evaluation does take place it rarely extends beyond subjective reports of enjoyment, personal satisfaction and individual learning.

Platform Completeness Check 6 - No Process

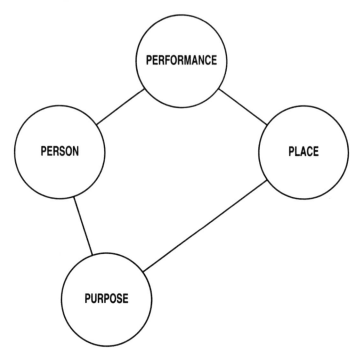

Lack of consideration of Process in formulating strategies for management development leads to a Platform that may demonstrate plenty of good intent, high hopes and even targets and objectives, but with little or no vision of how these will be fulfilled.

Our observation of a number of high-profile change initiatives provides all too common examples of this omission. High expectations are voiced by senior managers and often echoed in the demands of their direct reports. However, other than increasing the intensity of the demand, there is often little or no thought given to the Processes that are required in order to facilitate and accomplish the change. Words like 'empowerment' may be used in place of designed Processes - though 'abdication' may be closer to the reality experienced by managers 'on the ground'.

Snapshot

A radically new appraisal system was introduced. Managers felt very apprehensive and were looking for some training in this, since the way they handled it would be a factor in the assessment of their own managerial

Continued on next page

> *Continued from previous page*
>
> performance. The skills required for this new scheme were defined by the HR Manager and manuals were prepared. The General Manager, however, would not sanction the budget for training. He said, 'Anyone who has been promoted to a managerial position ought to be capable of carrying out appraisal. If they can't, they shouldn't be managers.'

Platform Completeness Check 7 - No Place

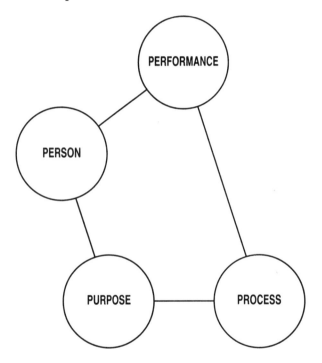

The omission of Place from the 5P Platform reveals a lack of consideration or clear definition of the context that is necessary and supportive of managerial performance and/or development.

With this omission the development approaches may well not take account of the real world context within which the participant operates, thus leading to potential problems with the transfer of the learning. The Process for development may be built on wrong assumptions of what the context is. This is likely to cause frustration or dissatisfaction amongst the participants in management development activities when they return to work with ideas that are unwelcome or unacceptable in the context of the culture, style, systems and other factors within their organisations.

Snapshot

A manager from a relatively small company attended a three-week general management course at a business school. She was asked by her Managing Director on her return whether is was worthwhile. Her response was that most of the participants were from larger corporations and everything kept being brought round to their issues and problems. 'They were not the sort of problems I am faced with and I found I was being forced to walk through a world I did not know most of the time. I found no value in this.'

Platform Completeness Check 8 - Platform skewed

The Critical Checks that we have carried out so far have looked at the dangers of the omission of a particular element from the 5P Platform. Equally damaging to the effectiveness of management development initiatives are the situations where a particular element is over-emphasised to the detriment of the other elements, resulting in a 'skewed' Platform.

Therefore the final Platform Completeness Check is concerned to ensure that each P has been appropriately considered and that the Platform is not overly driven from a particular perspective.

We have identified some possible 'skews' to the Model.

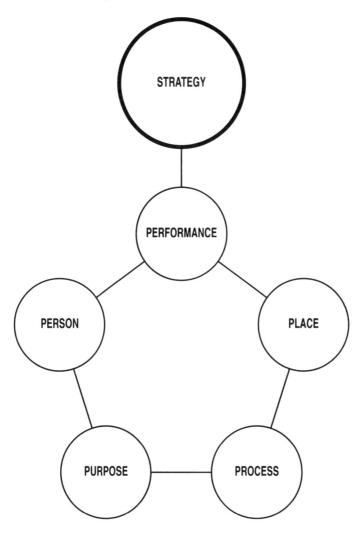

Strategically-driven management development
This is where the Strategic Hook is over-developed. We may find strong visions of where the organisation wants to be, but these are seen as remote and distant from the concrete, day-to-day nitty-gritty of what this means in terms of managers' performance requirements. As a result managers may come to view the strategic intentions of the organisation as abstract and unreal, and be unclear as to what they actually need to pay attention to if their work is to translate vision into reality.

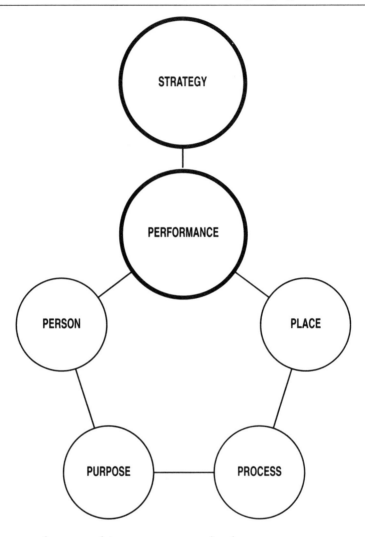

Business-performance-driven management development

Here there is a great emphasis on the strategic requirements of the organisation and on clearly communicated demands of what Performance these require of managers. However, there may be an over-preoccupation with output and bottom-line measures at the expense of adequate consideration of who the managers are, the Competencies they require, how they may be developed, and how the context is supportive of their endeavours.

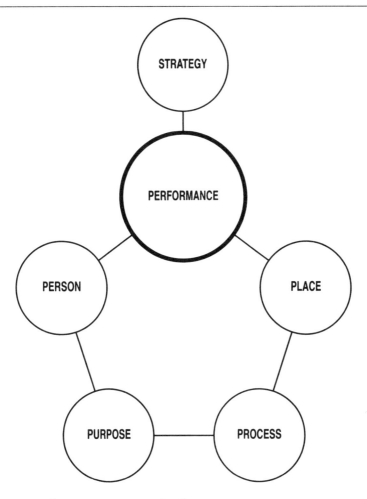

Performance-driven management development
Here the Performance element is over-emphasised and inadequately linked through to Strategy. The consequence is an overly tactical short-term focus that frequently degenerates into 'fire-fighting'. This orientation is often reflected in the nature of management development activities that are geared towards, at best, a 'quick fix' with little regard for the longer-term capability of the organisation.

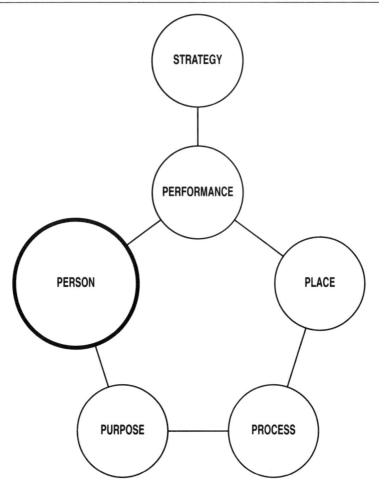

Person-driven management development

Here management development over-emphasises the Person - the manager and his or her Competencies and development potential. The development function, though often responsive, is overly person- and input-centred at the expense of performance and output, and little energy is invested in relating it to Performance needs. Where such needs are continuously made clear to everyone this situation may be acceptable, and can even be powerful, since it is likely to be more timely in its response to these needs than many bureaucratically driven approaches.

Snapshot

Extract from one company's Mission Statement: 'The company will assist and support all employees in developing to their maximum potential'.

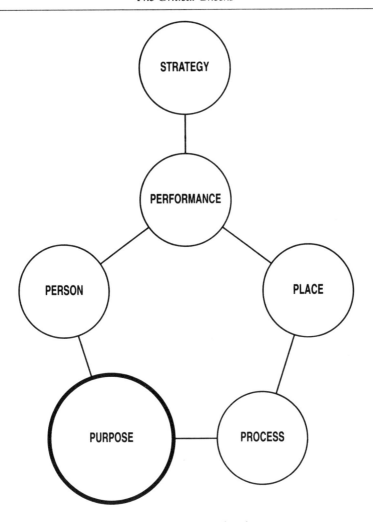

Development-objectives-driven management development

This 'skew' is where the Purpose is over-developed. Here enormous energy may be invested in setting the aims, goals and objectives (the 'what') of management development, so much so that the who, how, where and why are overlooked. Much of the systematic approach to training evidenced in the work of the old Training Boards displayed this pre-occupation - and many would argue that the mistake is being repeated by many of today's regulatory bodies. The consequence is often an apparently rational formulation of a framework for management development that looks fine on paper - but stays there!

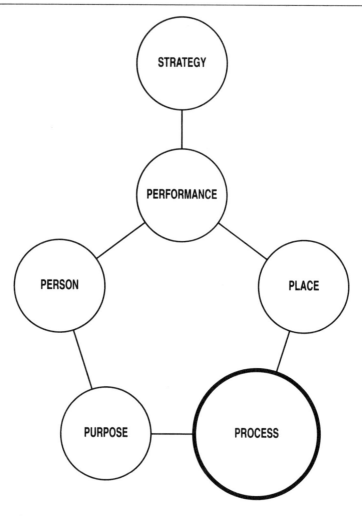

Process-driven management development

Here the 'skew' is towards Process - the 'how' of management development; the consequence is that means take over from ends. A preoccupation with the creation and display of often elegant and sophisticated learning processes (that evidence the skills of the trainer, facilitator or consultant, and often earn them the acclaim of their peers) takes attention away from who they are being designed for, and to what purpose. Even worse, the resulting processes may be alien to the organisational context and be seen as irrelevant to the real world performance requirements of the management cadre.

The buying into and adoption of the latest 'flavour of the month' approach or methodology can be equally symptomatic of a skew towards Process. All other considerations are cast aside in the fervour of conversion and advocation.

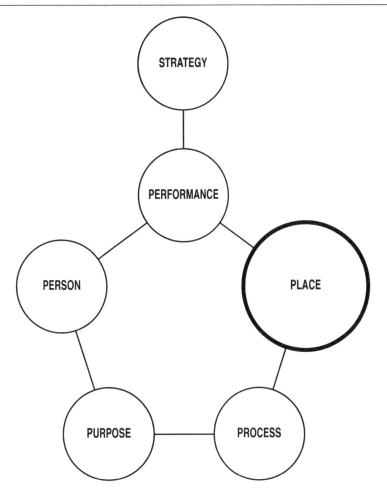

Place-driven management development

Here there is an inappropriate level of attention directed towards Place. Two sources of this 'skew' are commonly observable in organisations' thinking on management development. Firstly there is the emphasis on organisational design as the start point and end point of improvement initiatives. Thus the obsession with reorganisations, the introduction of new systems and procedures, etc, as almost a 'knee-jerk' response to demands for greater efficiency and effectiveness.

Little thought is given to the learning and development requirements posed by the new design, let alone as an alternative to changes to infrastructure.

The second route to a 'skewed' approach parallels the comments made in the previous section on Person. Thus we have been alarmed by the number of organisations that have bought into new approaches to organisations, whether to infrastructure or attempted culture change, which are rooted in the latest fad phenomenon or are ideologically rather than instrumentally based.

Summary

In Chapter 3 we focused on understanding the key elements that make up the 5P Platform of the Wadenhoe Model.

It would be easy to take away from this an impression of the Model as a vehicle for data collection. However, the use of the Critical Checks ensures that it becomes a dynamic vehicle for assisting decision-making and action. The value of these Checks is in applying rigour and thoroughness to our thinking about the formulation, design and delivery of management development.

The research identified that having collected information within the five P elements of Performance, Person, Purpose, Process and Place, it is essential that we then Check:

- The Completeness of the Model

- The Contents of each of the elements of the Model

- The Connections that link the elements and turn the Model into a stable structure

- The Construction of the Model and the extent to which it has been built up in a way that increases the probability of a successful intervention

- The Carrying-Out of the Model in terms of the way it is updated to continuously reflect the changing needs of the organisation.

Within this Chapter we have focused on the Checks for Completeness of the Model. We have looked specifically at the implications of any one of the five P elements being absent from our thinking about management development, and have looked at examples of these omissions to see what they tell us.

We have also looked at the potential for our thinking about management development to be 'skewed', by which we mean that one or other of the P elements has assumed undue importance in our thinking. This may lead to our management development activities appearing to follow the framework of the Model, while in reality there is an imbalance that continues to diminish the potential for our management development interventions to be strategically effective.

Chapter 5 now looks in detail at the remaining four Cs, ie the four Critical Checks for Content, Connection, Construction and Carrying-Out.

Checklist for Chapter 4

● Have each of the P elements a valid place in your thinking about management development? Do you have the right information for each of these?

● Is any of the information put on hold or discreetly ignored because of political considerations?

● Are any of the P elements of the 5P Platform over-developed or given undue weight in your decisions about management development? For example, is there a preoccupation with output and bottom-line measures? Is management development short term and 'fire-fighting' in nature? Is there a 'flavour of the month' approach to development?

● Is there a clear understanding of the strategy of the organisation that the managerial performance is intended to deliver?

● Is management performance clearly defined and understood in the organisation?

● Are individuals' needs taken into account in designing a management development event or in determining who should attend?

● Are the development objectives for each activity clearly defined and understood?

● Is sufficient thought given to the processes that are required in order to facilitate and accomplish change in your organisation?

● Is consideration given to the context that is necessary for and supportive of managerial performance and development?

Chapter 5
'THE STRUCTURE UNDER THE MICROSCOPE' - PLATFORM CONTENT CHECKS

Introduction

This Chapter is devoted to the second category of Critical Checks - that of Content.

Having assured ourselves that all the five Ps in the 5P Platform for management development are being appropriately considered, the next step is to Check on the critical features within each individual P element.

With this in mind, the aim is that by the end of this Chapter you should be able to:

● Critically assess the available information relating to each of the Ps using the Platform Content Checklist.

● Identify the need for further information, action and decision-making relating to the formulation of a viable management development initiative for the organisation.

Critical Checks - Platform Content

The purpose of the Platform Content Check is to sort and scrutinise the information in relation to issues that have been identified from our research as being critical to the effectiveness of management development approaches. Each Check within the Critical Content Checklist has also been labelled with a word beginning with the letter C, the intention being that the word used captures the essence of the Check.

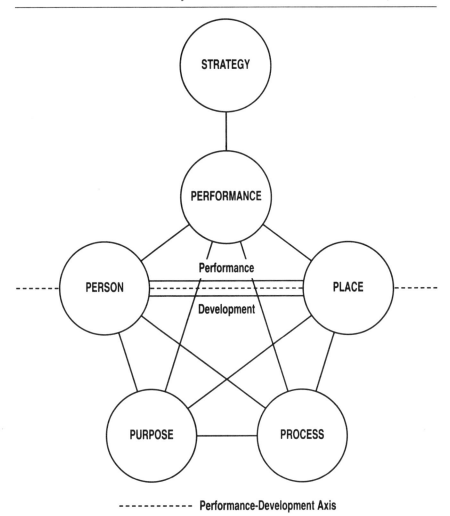

----------- **Performance-Development Axis**

Platform Content Check 1 - Performance
The Critical Content Checks for the Performance element of the Model are:

Competence Domains
What are the areas of activity in which managers are required to give their attention and perform? Have these Domains been clearly identified and have their current and required changed states been diagnosed?

Criteria
Have the necessary standards of performance within the Domains been identified and agreed?

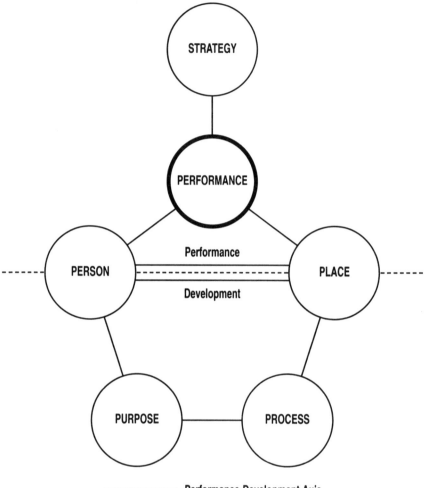

Centrality

Which of the identified Domains are the key foci for performance excellence and are core areas of activity in respect of the delivery of the business strategy of the organisation?

In our research we found widely differing interpretations of the term Performance and of the use of Competence Domains as a means of defining Performance.

We also found that there was often no framework to ensure that sufficient rigour was applied for an adequate understanding of Performance before any form of development took place.

Defining Competence Domains helps to transcend some of the traditional boundaries between Technical and Managerial Performance.

The definition of Competence Domains that we are using is as follows:

- Competence Domains refer to areas of activity regarded as important foci for performance excellence. They define key concerns to which managers need to pay particular attention and address. They define key performance areas in which the manager needs to contribute, eg profitability, risk, markets, competitors, customers, company standing, cash, quality, efficiency, innovation, staff development, suppliers, etc. These are all areas in which expertise needs to be applied if the organisation is to achieve its strategic ambitions.

Thus for Performance to be defined in terms that are useful we believe that the Competence Domains required for success must be identified and clarified for different levels in the organisation and, where appropriate, for different departments or functions.

This definition of Performance must not only include a precise identification of the Domain but also an understanding of what qualifies as acceptable performance within the Domain and therefore of the Criteria that will be used to measure achievement of an acceptable standard.

The definition of Performance that we are using has immediately opened up further questions in terms of the extent to which the strategy of the organisation has been made explicit in a way that enables managers at all levels to understand how their performance contributes (or not!) to the strategic performance of the organisation. As we have shown earlier, this Strategic Hook into the Performance element of the Model is of vital importance.

We believe that the lack of this clear and unambiguous definition of Performance has been a major weakness in the design of management development programmes. Unless it is possible to articulate the Performance that the manager is required to attain at work both in terms of the Domains and the level of Performance that is required, the selected development event has only a random chance of contributing to this.

It is implicit within our understanding of the element of Performance that we are in a position to evaluate the current standards of performance that are actually being achieved against the standards that are required both now and in the future. This will enable us to define the 'gap' that development must address.

If there is no gap between the desired and the present performance, there are a whole new set of questions to be asked:

- Are we achieving the desired corporate performance? If we are, we might like to consider whether the overall corporate objectives are sufficiently ambitious to be motivational.

- Are we considering management development for reasons other than strategic performance? There may be legitimate reasons for this: it merely creates a different set of objectives for the development process. These objectives may then be related to long-term educational standards, or may be linked into the reward structure. Either way let us be explicit about this at the outset.

Is there an alternative scenario where there is no perceived gap between actual managerial performance and the desired performance, and yet the corporate performance is not acceptable? If this is the case, we may need to probe more deeply to establish whether the Competence Domains that are being used for evaluation and appraisal are Central to the performance of the organisation or whether we have missed a vital ingredient. From our experience a good number of management development initiatives tinker at the edges of managerial performance, working on the 'nice to haves' rather than on the key areas and blockages that are Central to performance achievement.

If this fails to throw up any anomalies, we then need to look at the quality of the evaluation of current performance. Despite many years of appraisal training the overall quality of appraisal carried out is appalling. Until appraisal is valued by line managers the quality of the information being generated will always be of questionable value, providing scope for errors and inaccuracy in the design of management development activities.

Snapshot

A cross-section of senior managers in a manufacturing company were in discussion about performance appraisal. These three observations summarise their views:

- 'I know appraisal should be the time for reviewing the job and extending the role, but in reality it is just about getting the form filled in.'

- 'We have to review what we are doing, but the appraisal process doesn't provide this opportunity in our company.'

- 'Appraisal here is just a process of looking at objectives and if you've failed on one you are regarded as having failed - full stop.'

Platform Content Check 2 - Person
The Critical Content Checks for the Person element of the Model are:

Competencies and Characteristics
What are the behaviours and the underpinning knowledge, skills, attitudes and personal attributes required of managers? Have these Competencies and Characteristics been clearly identified and have the current and required changed states been diagnosed?

Calibration
Are the Competencies and Characteristics of the managers subject to regular assessment and appraisal?

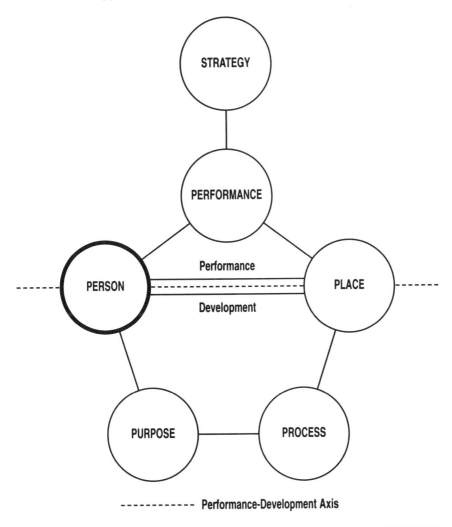

103

Communality

What is the similarity/diversity amongst the management cadre and has a view been formed of its nature and desirability?

To what extent should managers in the organisation require the same Competencies and Characteristics? Is it desirable that these should be similar whatever the level and function? And if so, what degree of similarity should exist?

To what extent does the organisation value the differences and clearly recognise the need for different Performances and different Competencies?

Snapshot

We were asked to design and deliver Assessment Centres for a Division within an international insurance group. The Division had gone through a reorganisation, creating a new hierarchy of roles, but the existing managers had already been allocated to the new roles.

Only when we fully explored the Competencies and Characteristics required and compared them with those possessed by the managers that had been appointed did the organisation recognise that with few exceptions they had the wrong people in post.

The Division performed poorly and was subsequently merged into another part of the group. All the managers lost their jobs.

When we first started to develop our checklist of the information that we needed to know about each manager who is being considered for development, the list proved very extensive. It included professional, technical and managerial knowledge and skills; attitudes to the company, to the job, to development; personality characteristics and profiles; learning capabilities and styles; and demographics - age, sex, experience, social groupings, etc.

It quickly became apparent, however, that we were talking about individual managers in two different contexts:

1 We were looking at the individuals in terms of their potential to perform in the desired way, and

2 We were looking at them as potential candidates on a development programme.

It was apparent that we needed to look at the information within the element of Person in two bites.

Person element above the Performance-Development Axis
Here the consideration of the element of Person relates to the managerial performance that is required and the status of the manager's Competencies and Characteristics in being able to deliver on these requirements.

Our examination of Performance earlier should have identified the 'gap' that exists between the manager's current performance and that required by the organisation. The question, then, is 'Why should this gap exist?'.

Are individuals lacking in some or all of the skills, knowledge or attitudes needed for performance? Are they temperamentally unsuited to perform in the desired way? Does the required performance clash with their values?

The Person element of the 5P Platform requires that we have an accurate understanding of the **Competencies and Characteristics** that relate to Performance in the agreed Domains.

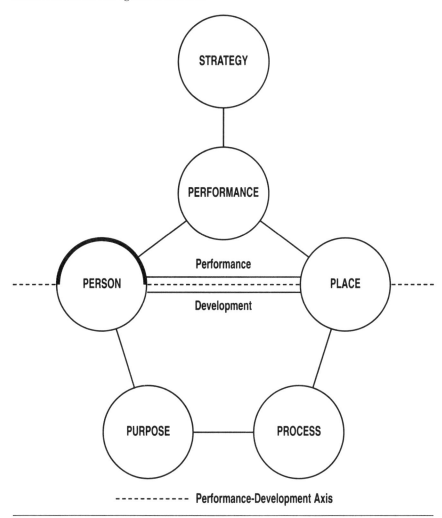

It is then essential that we have accurate and objective assessment and appraisal of individual managers' current Competencies and Characteristics in relation to those required for Performance in the agreed Domains. In our terms this means that the managers' Competencies have been **Calibrated**.

Our Critical Check is concerned therefore with the process though which this Calibration has taken place. We expressed our concern earlier about the quality and rigour of appraisal in many organisations. This suggests that accurate and objective Calibration may require considerable effort by management development practitioners to satisfy this Critical Check. In so doing we also need to check for similarity and diversity, ie for **Communality** of Competencies.

Widespread interest in the 1980s in McKinsey's '7S' framework for strategic analysis prompted many organisations to consider the 'shared values' required by the organisation for strategic success. As with so many good management ideas, this initial appeal became tarnished by the difficulties of carrying the ideas through in practise, and subsequently the idea has been dismissed as a fad. This is a pity, because these values feed into certain Competencies and Characteristics that are required across all managers and employees, ie there is a requirement for Communality.

Equally, in other areas it may be recognised that a single, imposed way of performing is restricting and greater individual freedom should be allowed - a further consideration under our Critical Check for Communality.

Person element below the Performance-Development Axis

Here again we are considering the element of Person, but this time the Person below the Performance-Development Axis. The Critical Check words are the same, ie we are checking for:

● Competencies and Characteristics

● Calibration, and

● Communality

Under the Check of **Competencies and Characteristics** we are obviously looking at the impact of these on the individual's approach to Development rather than to Performance. This is where we need to look, for example, at issues of learning style.

What are the behaviours and the underpinning skills, attitudes and personal attributes required for the manager to develop in the desired way? Have these Competencies and Characteristics been clearly identified, and has the manager's current state against each of these been adequately diagnosed?

Are these Competencies and Characteristics subject to regular assessment and

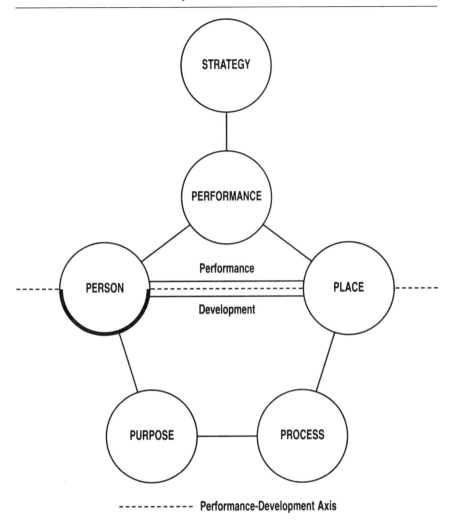

---------- **Performance-Development Axis**

appraisal - are they **Calibrated**? The same concerns about accuracy and objectivity also apply here.

Is there a sense of **Communality** of these Competencies and Characteristics between the managers to be developed, ie are they all the same? And if so, what is the implication for the necessary development?

What is likely to be their attitude to development? Have they, for example, the necessary numeracy or literacy to handle the development that is required? How mature will they be within a development process?

We are referring therefore to the personal characteristics of the manager in terms of psychographics and demographics. Have their personality profiles, learning styles, orientation to change, career stage, age, background, etc, been taken into account before the investment in any form of development is considered?

Snapshot

Over the decades when the company had a strong technological edge over all its competitors, its strategy was to manufacture as much of its product as possible while maintaining an exceptionally high quality standard. Management development effort was focused on first line managers - the supervisors - since they of all the management ranks most influenced quality and quantity. Eight main areas of managerial performance common to all supervisors whatever their department and function were identified and assessment centres were used for selection using these as their criteria. This Communality was recognised as a strong contributor to the business success of the company.

However, when the company lost this technological advantage and rapid response to customer requirements became the basis of their new business strategy, the focus for development shifted to more senior levels. Core values about quality and customer focus remained important, but more scope for individuality was allowed across the senior management ranks.

Platform Content Check 3 - Purpose

The Critical Content Checks for the Purpose element of the Model are:

'Causes' or Development Objectives

What are the aims, goals and objectives for management development? Have they been clearly identified?

Criticality

Are the management development objectives Critical in the sense of being cardinal to the strategy of the organisation and, if not carried out, will lead to crisis? Do they tackle the real causes of poor performance rather than the symptoms?

Currency

Would the management development initiative that tackles these 'Causes' be timely? Is the Purpose Current rather than being either out of date or even premature. Is it opportune in responding to, or riding on the waves of, 'live issues'?

Our research shows that on many occasions an instant solution creeps into the decision-making process when it comes to deciding what the development programme should address. How often have we heard 'We want a team-building programme' . . . 'It's all about leadership' . . . 'The trouble is that none of them will make a decision'. The die is cast and a decision has been made about the content

---

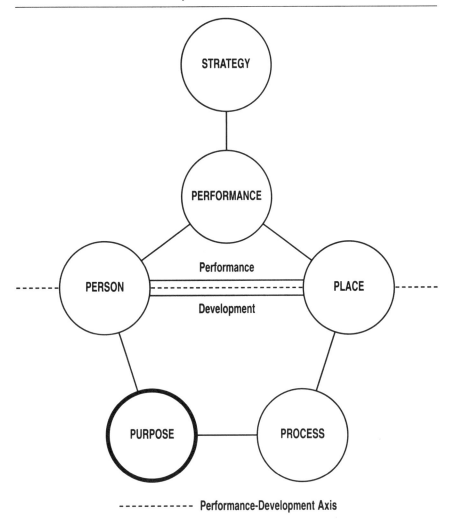

------------ Performance-Development Axis

of the development programme without going through the stage of declaring the Development Objectives.

The Purpose element of the Model requires that we make explicit the desired outcomes from the programme, and in particular the Development Objectives. It is a sad reflection that despite decades of management training there is still a general inability to write an effective objective.

A common trend from our research is that the **'Causes'** or Development Objectives of a particular event are:

● poorly defined where they exist at all

● ill-understood by the tutors who are offering the event, and

- rarely made explicit to the participants even when they are understood.

Even with the Development Objectives defined, our Critical Checks require that further questions be asked.

Recently time has become an ever scarcer commodity and there is little sign of the situation changing much in the near future. Time spent on development is one of the casualties of the increasing managerial pressure. For participants to feel positive and enthusiastic about dedicating time to a development process it must be seen that its focus is correct and that addressing the issues concerned is perceived as **Critical** - Critical to the organisation and Critical to their own success.

The other question that is frequently asked is whether this is the right time to be making the investment. This is a valid question, but one that can only be answered by the managers and the organisation itself in terms of the **Currency** of the development objectives, ie their timeliness. Can the development be postponed and delivered at a time when it is more relevant, or indeed has its relevance already passed? We see major programmes being run in organisations that were designed for needs that existed two or three years earlier, but because the programme was popular then it is maintained and run unchanged. It may be that the set of needs for which it was intended remain Current and important, but it is essential that this Currency is checked.

Platform Content Check 4 - Process

The element that we call Process is concerned with the identification and development of content and process. Therefore the Critical Content Checks for the Process element of the Model are:

'Courses of Action' or Development Content and Methodology

What are the approaches and processes for development? Have they been identified and planned? Does the design tell a coherent story? Is it tailored rather than a 'cook book'?

Celerity

Will the process of development be completed within the necessary time frame? Is the speed of the process realistic?

Critical mass

Will the number of managers participating in the development process be sufficient to achieve a critical mass? Will an adequate proportion of the management cadre be covered by the proposed process?

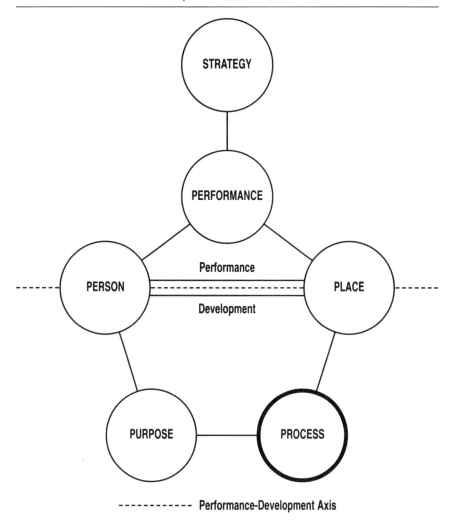

------------ **Performance-Development Axis**

Many management development initiatives seem to start with a preoccupation with the content that must be covered rather than looking at the combination of process and content. Or the process has been taken for granted - 'We want a course' - and the organisation has in addition worked out exactly how the five days of their course will be spent. The balance and weighting of the topics is driven more by the slots available between meal breaks than by any consideration of what is really required.

Equally we see a preoccupation with particular processes irrespective of the content to be covered. This appears to be particularly prevalent with outdoor development. Some of this is the tendency for 'flavour of the month' approaches, but a worrying part from our perspective is the apparent lack of will to recognise and assess the alternatives.

Snapshot

A Training Manager was expounding on the type of course he wanted for his managers. 'I went to a seminar on employment law. It was run by an MP who is also a barrister. What an orator - he would pick on people and quite unmercifully put them on the spot! That made us sit up and pay attention. That is the sort of thing that we need.'

Regularly we find people who are involved in management development who lack an understanding of learning as a process. Yet we believe that it is an essential requirement for designing and running events as well as for considering some of the wider issues. This can lead to an unwillingness to think beyond the established solutions that seems to pervade many of the organisations in our research.

Snapshot

Professor in a major business school: 'I have been using this case method since I experienced it at Harvard some twenty years ago. I liked it as a student and I must admit that I have not stopped since to think about its relevance to the way I teach. Recently I have been disturbed by reading about other methods that seem to have more validity, particularly since some of these have been endorsed by people from Harvard. I really do have a need to update myself.'

Our Critical Check questions for **'Courses of Action'** therefore examine whether consideration has been given to alternative methods of achieving the development objectives. As you will recall from our earlier comments we are concerned that the methods used for development should recognise that a crucial part of the process of learning takes place in the workplace. The Process consideration needs to take this into account. Development is often a long-term activity and therefore the process is likely to need continuity over an extended period. Rarely is it possible to consider each Development Objective in isolation.

Our Check on 'Courses of Action' also needs to test therefore that the various parts of the selected development process make up a cohesive whole. Obvious examples of a lack of cohesion are the long development programmes often offered by the major business schools that have three or four days of personal development often involving some form of physical activity that sit uncomfortably within a classroom-dominated programme. Each on their own is legitimate and may be appropriate, but they do not work well together as a cohesive whole.

Finally, of course, the selected process must retain an element of flexibility in order to accommodate the issues that will inevitably emerge as the participants engage in the process.

We also need to carry out the Critical Checks of **Celerity** and **Critical Mass**. There has been a steady reduction in the duration of 'courses' over recent years. Where once a general management programme of six or eight weeks' duration was the norm, these have been shortened and shortened.

Organisations do not find the speed with which the development is taking place (**Celerity**) acceptable. Similarly organisations have embarked on action learning programmes only to become disenchanted and dissatisfied by the length of time that elapses before they see results.

So the Check for Celerity is concerned with ensuring that the organisation does not develop totally ungrounded and unrealistic expectations of how long it will take to achieve learning and development and to see the results feeding through into observable behaviour change and bottom-line performance improvement. This is a particular concern with large culture change initiatives where for a large organisation with established traditions the change process needs to be measured in years rather than weeks. At the individual level the processes of transition do not happen overnight. They require time for 'letting go' before there can be real 'moving on'.

Equally the Check for Celerity is concerned with the appropriateness of the selected development process where the organisation has time scales that must be met. A long-term educational process is clearly inappropriate where the organisation has a short-term skills development need in order to avoid bankruptcy.

Snapshot

At a recent meeting the Human Resources Director of a major engineering company declared: 'Our business plan changes dramatically every year, so a development process that takes 18 months is useless to me. I want something that produces results this year.'

The third check is for **Critical Mass**. The concern here is with the situation where the management cadre are lined up twelve at a time to attend a series of programmes. Very often the potential benefits to the first group are long gone by the time the last group emerges from the process. Similarly we have observed the often naive assumption that we need only send one person from each department on the course, and that he or she will then pass on the learning to the rest.

By contrast we have seen the impact where the whole company is exposed to a concept or where the development focus is on the whole of a department or real team. The concern therefore within this check for Critical Mass is whether a sufficient number of managers will be experiencing the development process to ensure that there is a real momentum to change that is sustainable.

Platform Content Check 5 - Place

The Critical Content Checks for the Place element of the Model are:

'Culture' (psycho-social)

Have the organisational culture, climate, conventions and customs necessary for mobilisation of managerial performance and development been identified and put in place?

We need to examine whether the aspects of Culture that we are considering are actually Confirmatory of that performance and development. Does espoused theory consistently match with actual practise?

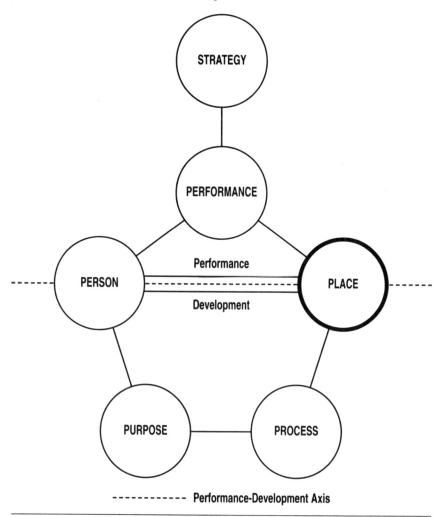

------------ Performance-Development Axis

Is that Performance Championed, and is this championing evident within the power structure?

Components (physical/structural)
Have the physical environment and facilities, and the organisation structures and systems necessary for mobilisation of managerial performance and development, been clearly identified and put in place?

Convenient
Are the physical environment and facilities and the structures and systems Convenient for performance and development? Are the necessary resources accessible? Is the environment amenable and supportive to performance *and* development?

As with our consideration of the element of Person, there was a tendency to try to include too much under the heading of Place and, like the approach to Person, the breakthrough came as we recognised that we need to look at issues in the environment from two orientations. First there is the need to consider Place as the arena for managerial Performance. Second, Place needs to be addressed as the context for managerial Development.

Our definition of management development is **'A Planned and Purposeful Process that enables managers' Performance in their Place of work'**. Implicit within this definition is that Development has not occurred until it results in a change of Performance at work.

We have also found it helpful to separate the psychological and social aspects of the environment (the 'Culture') from the physical and structural aspects (Components).

Place element above the Performance-Development Axis
Here therefore we are considering Place in the arena of managerial Performance.

In considering **'Culture'** we are asking questions about the way in which the social and psychological environment in the organisation impacts on the willingness or the ability of managers to perform in the ways and to the standards that are being demanded.

Every organisation has its rites and rituals, its war stories and its heroes that combine to reinforce 'the way we do things around here'. Before we embark on any management development process it is important that there is a clear understanding of these and the impact that they might have on the way that managers perform. Fear is a strong aspect of many organisational Cultures. Often the fear may be historic and based on a particular piece of top management behaviour. But if that fear results in an unwillingness to risk failure, this is of major importance if the organisation claims to want more entrepreneurial managers.

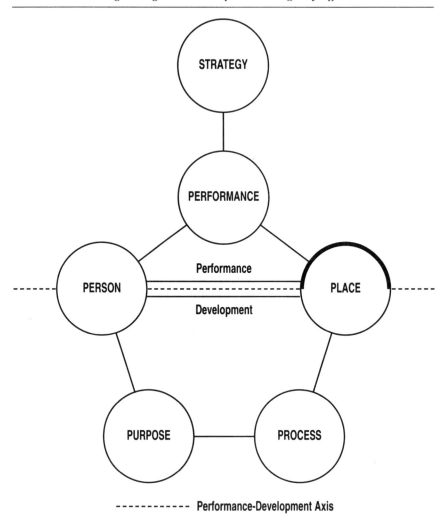

- - - - - - - - - - - Performance-Development Axis

Similarly we have observed organisations where the top management espouse certain behaviours but behave differently themselves - 'Do as I say, not as I do'. Here they may be seen to Champion the desired performance change, but their own performance fails to Confirm what is really required.

Snapshot

An organisation recently ran a programme with the express intent of encouraging managers to participate more in the way that they manage. When a promotion opportunity emerged there was an ideal opportunity

Continued on next page

Continued from previous page
to Confirm the importance of the behaviour by promoting an appropriate role model. However, it was the arch-autocrat who was promoted. Where was the Confirming behaviour from the organisation to help individuals to perform in a different way?

Similarly we need to check on the **Components** of the environment and the extent to which they make it **Convenient** for managers to perform in the required manner.

Snapshot

Managers in a distribution operation were being required to do more planning and also to conduct better appraisals. None of the managers had individual offices and their shared office was a glass box overlooking the warehouse. Anyone sitting down was clearly visible and assumed to be doing nothing. Not very Convenient.

The Checks for Components and Convenience are concerned with the structures and systems that exist in the organisation and the extent to which they enable or disable managerial performance. Therefore we need to consider the Place in which the performance is required and determine whether the performance is likely within the bounds of the existing Culture, systems and style, both physical and emotional. This consideration may lead to a view that development is not the answer; that the managers are not lacking in skills, knowledge or attitude but that some changes need to be made to other aspects of the organisation before individuals will be motivated to perform in the desired way.

Place element below the Performance-Development Axis
As with our consideration of Person above and below the Performance-Development Axis, the Critical Checks for Place are the same above and below the line. Thus below the Performance-Development Axis we also need to consider aspects of

● 'Culture'

● **Components** and

● **Convenient**

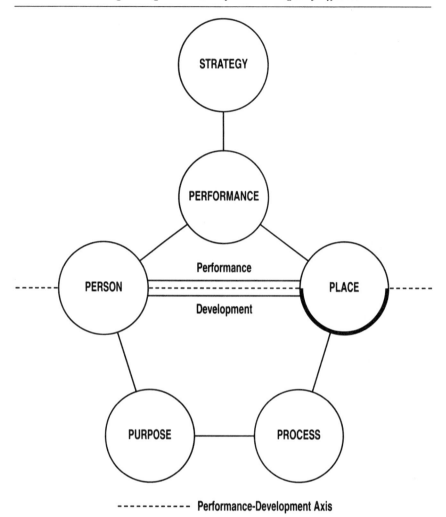

STRATEGY

PERFORMANCE

Performance

PERSON — — — — — — — — — — — — — — — — PLACE

Development

PURPOSE   PROCESS

- - - - - - - - - - - Performance-Development Axis

Within the Check that we call **'Culture'** we are considering the impact of the social and psychological environment on the willingness and ability of managers to develop. We recognise, for example, the importance of reflection and review in the process of learning; these are activities that need time to execute effectively. Yet we frequently hear from managers that they do not have time to think! In many organisations managerial life is about being busy. Within this culture time spent on reflection and review would be seen as wasted.

So we are concerned with the extent to which the psychological and social environment is conducive to learning and development. Do the actions match the words? Do managers preach learning but not allow time for learning on the job? Are people sent on courses with no briefing on why they are going nor any debriefing about what they have learned?

Do the senior managers in the organisation support and Champion the process of development? Through their own behaviour do they Confirm the importance of the development?

Equally we have seen organisations where neither junior nor middle managers have their own office or even their own desk. The Components of the organisation are not Convenient for the process of learning. Anyone spending time in the office is not considered to be managing!

Snapshot

A very large manufacturing organisation with similar operations on many sites throughout the world wanted to increase the co-operation between the different country managers and in particular wanted them to learn from each other's experience. Yet they were each on individual performance bonus schemes that potentially represented 25 per cent of their salaries and each month a 'league table' of plant performance was published. There was considerable competition generated between the plants. The managers involved would have liked to learn from their 'rivals', but were scared of revealing any secrets of their success!

Summary

These then are the Critical Checks that need to be made on the Content of each of the P elements of the 5P Platform for management development success.

Time and again our research identified situations where the failure to check on the Content of each of the elements of the Platform had sown the seeds for eventual under-achievement or downright failure of the management development initiatives.

You will have seen from the 'snapshots' examples of:

● failure to identify key Performance areas and objectives leading to development work that the managers found irrelevant to where they believed the organisation was going

● inadequate diagnosis of the necessary managerial Competencies leading to development work that was unfocused and unnecessary

● unclear definition of the Development Objectives that are really required to tackle critical and timely blockages to Performance

- inadequate effort being put into the design of learning activities leading to Processes that are not effective and that the managers find hard to accept

- insufficient attention paid to the organisational context for Performance and Development leading to development activities that do not result in a change in managerial performance at work

- initiatives being jeopardised because influential and powerful people have not attended

As always we are concerned not to criticise the instigators of management development initiatives for these failures, but to provide a rigorous and comprehensive framework for handling the mass of data that informs the strategic effectiveness of management development.

As a working document we have included a list of the Critical Check questions (the 'Cs') at the end of this Chapter. We have already emphasised the need for you to take these 'Generaliseable and Simple' questions and apply your own Accuracy. Add your own Critical Check questions, and if you feel that there are any aspects that we have omitted, let us know. . . The research continues!

Critical Checks for Chapter 5

Performance
- What are the areas of activity in which managers are required to give their attention and perform? Have these Domains been clearly identified? Have the managers' current and required changed states in respect of these Domains been diagnosed?

- Which of the Competence Domains are key foci for managerial performance excellence and core areas of activity in respect of delivery of the organisation's strategy?

- Have the necessary standards and outcomes of managerial performance within the Domains been identified and benchmarked?

Person
- What are the underpinning knowledge, skills, attitudes and personal attributes that are required for managers to perform in the agreed Domains? Have they been clearly identified and have the current and required changed states been accurately diagnosed?

- Are the Competencies and Characteristics of managers subject to regular assessment and appraisal?

- What is the similarity/dissimilarity amongst the management cadre, and has a view been formed of its nature and desirability?

Purpose
- What are the aims, goals and objectives for management development? Have they been clearly identified?

- Is the achievement of these Development Objectives critical in the sense of being cardinal and, if not met, likely to lead to crisis in the organisation? Do they tackle the causes rather than the symptoms?

- Is the management development initiative timely? Is the purpose current rather that out of date or premature? Is it opportune in responding to a live issue?

Process
- What are the approaches and Processes for development? Have they been planned taking all the other elements into account? Does the design tell a story? Is the design tailored rather than being taken 'off the shelf'?

- Will the Process of development be completed within the necessary time-frame? Is the time necessary for the Process to have the desired impact realistic?

- Will there be sufficient managers participating in the development initiative to create a Critical Mass? Do the managers/Directors who hold the real power to influence implementation feature amongst these?

Place
- Have the Culture, climate, conventions and customs necessary for the mobilisation of managerial performance and development been identified and put in place? Are they Confirmatory of the performance and development? Is the espoused theory consistently matched by actual practise?

- Do the Directors and senior managers who hold power in the organisation Champion and demonstrate their commitment through their observable behaviour?

- Have the physical environment and facilities and the organisation's structures and systems for mobilisation of managerial Performance and Development been identified and put in place? Are they Convenient for Performance and Development? Are the necessary resources accessible? Is the infrastructure amenable and supportive?

Chapter 6
'INSPECTING THE RIGGING - CHECKING THE CONNECTIONS AND CROSS-BRACING

Introduction

So far in our consideration of the Wadenhoe Model we have looked at the different elements of the 5P Platform and checked on the presence of, and appropriate emphasis on, each P - the Critical Check for Platform Completeness. Further, we have looked within each P to Check that adequate consideration has been given to the Critical Content variables.

However, the Platform is as yet far from being the fully formed template required for effective management development initiatives. Beyond consideration of the individual elements of the Model, we now need to consider their Connectivity.

Many management development initiatives are less than successful because the various ingredients, and the choices and decisions made about them, while sound in their own right, do not 'stack up' as a whole. Often the resultant activities not only fail to be mutually reinforcing, but are contradictory. For example, the development methods chosen, while of proven use in some forms of management development, may be manifestly inappropriate to the particular objectives of the case in hand.

The consequence of a lack of Connectivity is that the interventions are likely to fail - and even fly apart - on implementation. It is important, therefore, that a template for management development not only contains the essential ingredients, but that these ingredients are mutually compatible, and are supporting and

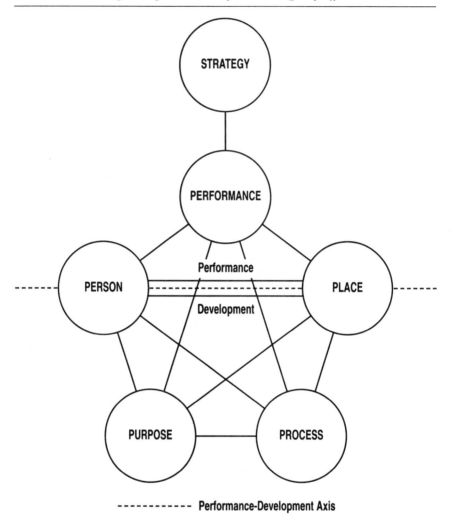

---------- **Performance-Development Axis**

reinforcing of each other. The need is to create a 'structure' that has a wholeness and an integrity, that provides sturdiness and resilience to the development initiative. These qualities are achieved by building linkages across the elements of the 5P Platform. Such linkages are achieved through the consideration of a series of Connection Checks, which build on the already described Completeness and Content Checks.

- ● **Platform Completeness**

- ● **Platform Content**

- ● **Platform Connection**

The aims of this Chapter are:

- to demonstrate the importance of the Connections that give the Model its integrity and wholeness, and

- to provide the key question that must be asked in respect of each of the Connections

Critical Connection Checks

Before looking at the Connection Checks in detail let us show what we mean by an element existing in isolation without any sense of connection or cohesion. The snapshots provide two examples.

Snapshots
A lack of Connection between Strategy and Performance:
In a public sector organisation the business strategy was very closely guarded by the Chief Executive. He had clear targets and objectives in mind against which his Executives should perform, but his sense of secrecy and resistance to sharing the strategy prevented him from communicating these. As a result much money was spent on the development of these Executives without them having an understanding of what they were required to achieve.

A lack of Connection between Purpose and Place:
Responsibility for creating a development programme for the Partners of a professional practise was delegated by the Managing Partner to the Personnel function. The focus of the programme was on building a more cohesive and strategic thinking 'firm'. In the 24 hours preceding the programme as many as half of the Partners scheduled to attend withdrew, quoting 'client needs'. They were able to quote in detail the cost in client chargeable hours of them attending the programme. The Personnel professional was not valued in this environment and therefore the Purpose of the programme was not 'Championed'.

Connections Around the Outside of The Model

In this part of the Chapter each of the Connections is described in detail, starting with those around the outside of the Platform.

Performance to Person Connection - Capability
The Critical Check question to be asked here is:

● Is there a match between Competencies (managers' abilities to perform) and Competence Domains (required performance areas)?

In other words, does the capability profile of the management cadre align with

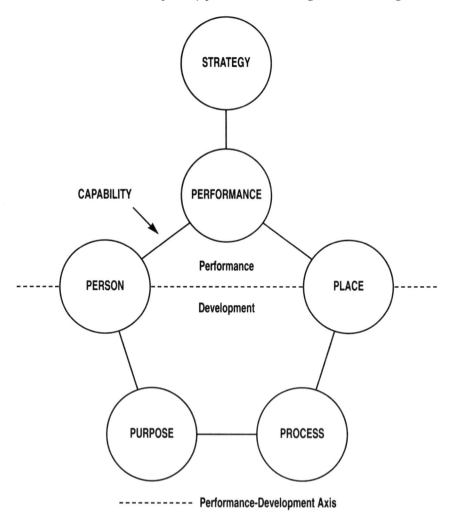

the key concerns and performance areas that managers need to address? If the managers were to develop the Competencies and Characteristics that have been identified, will they then be Capable of performing in the manner required by the organisation?

In the worst case scenario, for example, the managers' skills and qualities (while perhaps impressive in themselves) may be inappropriate for, or may have become redundant to, both the current and emergent performance requirements of the organisation.

Thus, an organisational shift in focus towards core business - and consequent outsourcing - requires that managers develop skills of contracting and project-managing work that is now being resourced from outside suppliers. These are very different skills from those required for directly managing a team of internal employees.

The Connection Check for Capability is therefore looking at the current and potential future match between Person and Performance - is development likely to make the individual Capable of performing in the way and to the standard that the organisation requires?

Much work has been done within the Management Charter Initiative and by other bodies and authorities to develop standard lists of Competencies for various management roles and positions. These can provide useful guidelines for starting the analysis process, but great care needs to be taken not to follow them blindly with the consequent creation of a set of criteria that have little relevance for the needs of the business.

Snapshots

1

After development work with the Executives of a UK PLC we were invited to spend a day with the Board of Directors looking at their personal management styles. The organisation was growing rapidly internationally and the new strategy required a high level of delegation and trust. At the end of the day the Operations Director put his head in his hands and said very bravely, 'I now know what is required of me and I can't do it. It is so alien to the way I have always operated that I don't feel capable of behaving in that way nor inclined to put the effort into trying.'

The organisation was then able to manage his move from the organisation to a highly respected post elsewhere with dignity and integrity.

2

A set of competencies used for management development purposes in a large company included 'Imagination'. A senior accountant, whose role

Continued on next page

Continued from previous page

carried considerable managerial responsibility, was criticised for not being imaginative. He said, 'I cannot see how this is relevant to my job. My work in finance is structured and there are very clear rules to be followed. This is the job - implementing financial control and evaluation systems. Being imaginative is not part of the way I am expected to work and indeed it could be counter-productive. I would like to know how it was determined that this is important for my work.'

Person to Purpose Connection - Capacity

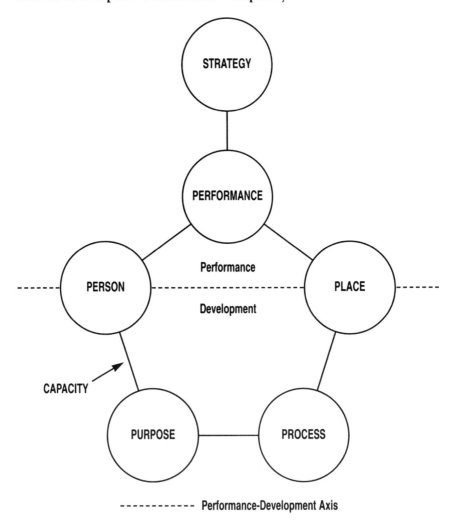

Performance-Development Axis

We are now looking at a Connection below the Performance-Development Axis. Therefore our focus here is on the people to be Developed in a particular Competency or Characteristic.

The Critical Check questions to be asked here are:

- Is there latent potential within managers to develop further?

- What is their trainability?

- Do the development objectives match the people at whom they are targeted?

Snapshots

A company operating in a field of information technology grew rapidly both in the numbers employed and in the volume of business. The Chairman and the Managing Director found that they were sucked into the day-to-day management of the company and the supervision of employees at the cost of not having space to deal with the broader issues of business development. They appointed to the first real managerial roles eight employees who had joined the company in its early days as programming specialists. After a short time it was obvious that they were not performing as managers and a modular development programme was arranged for them.

The declared objectives of the development programme were focused on developing their man-management abilities. Issues addressed included communication, motivation and leadership.

After three modules in a six-month period it was apparent that they were not taking the managerial initiatives that were expected of them. Discussions with each of them, using data from a personality inventory as the basis for the conversation, revealed that six of the eight were not likely to adapt naturally to managerial roles. They admitted that they really did not want to be managers and would prefer to be left in the specialist roles for which they had been engaged. Strong social reasons had prevented them from saying so earlier. No amount of development activity was likely to change this.

Just as we checked whether the individuals were Capable of achieving the performance that was required, we must ask here whether they have the Capacity to develop in the desired ways. Having defined the precise development objectives it is important to be realistic about the potential for each individual to develop the right Competencies. There may be Characteristics, such as amount or quality

---

of experience, personality, learning style, values and attitudes, that would prevent the development from bearing fruit, ie they lack the Capacity to develop in the way that is required.

Equally, in travelling down the route between Person and Purpose we may have distorted the focus of the Development Objectives. So the Check for Capacity is also concerned with testing and confirming whether achievement of the declared Development Objectives would affect the appropriate Competencies and Characteristics for a particular manager.

The final element of this Check is concerned with trainability of the individuals. We have checked that they have the Capacity to develop and that the Development Objectives are appropriate, but do the individuals actually have the will and the outlook to be developed?

Clearly we are not asking these questions for their own sake. If the answer to any of these Checks suggests that a development initiative would be wasted, then we would need other reasons for committing time and effort to those individuals. The organisation might still make a decision for the individuals concerned to go through a development programme with their peer group, but this would then be happening for social or motivational reasons rather than with the expectation of serious change taking place.

As with so much of what we are describing within the Model there is great benefit in making these issues explicit rather than going forward with unreal expectations.

Purpose to Process Connection - 'Can do'
The Critical Check questions to be asked here are:

● Is there a reasonable probability that the development process can deliver its objectives, ie that it is not unduly 'pie in the sky'?

● Is the process 'fit for purpose'?

We identified in Chapter 3 the danger of bias affecting the choice of development Process. We showed how these choices are often made very subjectively and are often based on personal experience; 'I did this business game and really enjoyed it - all our managers ought to go through the same' is a crude example of how this can happen.

Sometimes intuition or personal preference works, and the Process picked produces actions and results that meet the Development Objectives. The 'Can do' Check tests whether there is a sense that the Process is likely to achieve the desired development - is it the most appropriate for the Purpose?

Remember that at this stage we are still proceeding around the outside Connections of the Model. We have not considered whether this is the most appropriate Process in terms of the needs of the individual. We will return to this later.

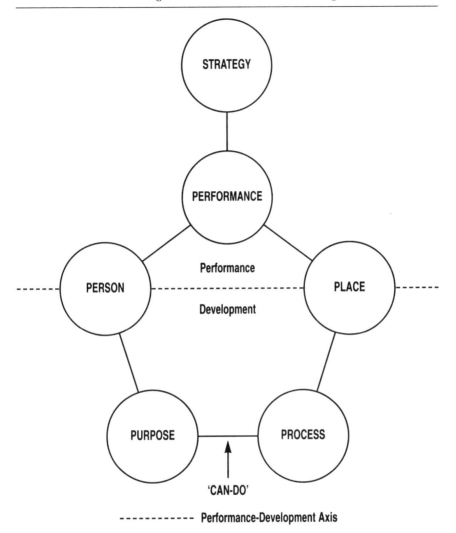

Performance-Development Axis

Snapshot

A four-day programme was run to help managers develop their skills in using a particular personality testing instrument. Pre-course material had been sent out to cover the knowledge aspects.

The majority of the programme time was classroom-based listening to lectures on 'how to do it'. There was little opportunity to put the ideas into practise and thereby to develop skills within the tutored environment.

Most of the participants left with fears about using the instrument for the first time in their real work environment.

One of the criticisms of management development providers is that they tend to promote the Process with which they are most familiar and confident. We know people who believe that Myers Briggs is an essential ingredient in every programme design. Similarly there are business schools where the case study is *de rigueur* '. . .if it's good enough for Harvard. . .!' There is a strong need therefore for organisations to understand the possible range of development and learning processes that are available so that they are in a position to identify the 'Can do' process for themselves.

Process to Place Connection - Conducive

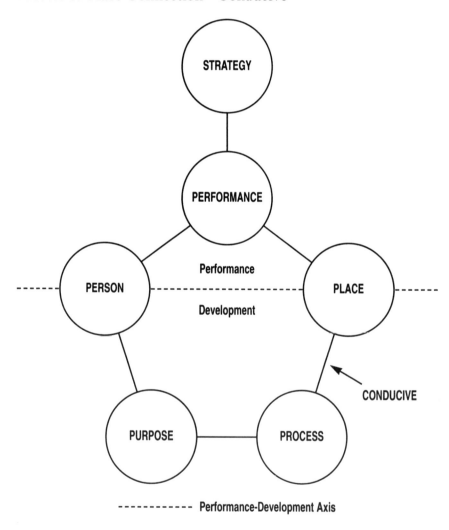

The Critical Check questions to be asked here are:

● Is the Place conducive to the development process?

● Is the context supportive of the Process?

As with the element of Person, that of Place has different meanings when considered above or below the Performance-Development Axis. Here we are considering the connection with Place in the Development arena below the Axis rather than the Performance arena. We are considering the Place in which Development is taking place.

If the chosen Development Process involves some off-site activity the element of Place becomes more complex in its concept. We will need to take account of both the venue for the off-the-job activity as well as the Development environment at the place of work. The questions we are asking along the Process to Place Connection are therefore concerned with whether the environment is Conducive to the process that is being considered.

Over the past ten years there has been an explosive growth in the number of hotels and specialist venues for running training programmes. From our own experience of running training programmes in hotels throughout the world it has to be said that very few of them genuinely understand the needs of people working on management development.

This lack of understanding can be as apparently simple as the degree of flexibility for meals and other refreshments, the quality of visual and other learning aids, or whether other events in the venue are intrusive. Or it could be a deeper issue such as the extent to which delegates believe they are in an environment in which they can talk safely about confidential issues that the programme is trying to address.

Snapshot

Six months after entering the company (a hotels and brewing chain), new graduates attended a one-week foundation management course at a residential training centre. On the first morning of the course one of them, speaking for the majority of course, said that this was like going back to school or college. It bore no resemblance to the place of work that they knew. They reacted against being forced to sit behind desks and listen with prescribed lunch and other breaks, ie those aspects of college life from which they felt they had escaped in going to work. From the start this seemed to reinforce a mind set that the programme would be irrelevant for their learning requirements.

Continued on next page

Continued from previous page

Later on in the week it became clear that many of them did not feel that their workplace, be it in the inns and restaurants or the breweries and offices, was very conducive to their development as managers. There was no private space in their work environment other than their cars! They also described a strong 'macho' culture in which uncertainty was classed as weakness.

In our experience there is rarely sufficient thought given to these aspects of the environment. The checklist that a secretary is given to try to find a suitable venue for a development event is likely to be more concerned with the size of the swimming pool (which in the event is rarely used) than with the process by which lunch is served and how far it is from the classroom to the syndicate rooms.

We have put this aspect of the Connection first as it tends to be very visible and is one of the hygiene factors that cannot improve the quality of the training if right but can detract significantly if it is wrong.

So this is one facet of our understanding of the Connection between Purpose and Place - is the environment in the venue Conducive to the proposed Process?

A deeper issue is the extent to which the environment at work is Conducive to the proposed Development Process, or to development at all.

Snapshot

The company had embarked on a programme of development for all its managers. The start of this was a series of off-the-job modules. In follow-up discussions with groups of employees one manager said, 'The Chief Executive has said publicly that if you are not a graduate you will not get on around here. I am not. Why should I bother to take this programme seriously?' Another supported this: 'He also said that if you have been here more than five years you can't have much ambition. I've been here eight.'

When this was put to the Chief Executive, he was surprised and said that his remarks had been taken out of context. However, whatever his intentions, few employees were prepared to believe that these remarks should not be taken seriously.

Action learning, for example, is a powerful development process but requires access to significant information if the participants are to make headway with the action from which they will learn. In a highly task-oriented organisation the culture may not allow people space to reflect on and review the learning that is emerging. Equally, junior managers may not have access to the strategic information that they require. Similarly such an apparently unstructured approach to development may leave the individual's line manager feeling very uncomfortable about his lack of control.

Further evidence of a working environment that is not Conducive to the desired Development is captured in the following snapshot.

Snapshot

A young manager was rated by his company as having potential for development:
'I find myself intolerant of the mediocrity of much middle and senior management. They appear to be people of astonishingly low ability who rather than harnessing creative and intellectual capability in young people seek to squash it through directive and restrictive managerial styles.'

We also of course have examples of the opposite.

Snapshot

A junior manager in a financial service company:
'I had been attending my professional course on day release for a year when my new manager asked to see me about it. My first thought was 'What's gone wrong?', since this had never happened before. She spent an hour going over what I had learned, relating this to my development needs from my last appraisal and how we could use this in the way I managed my section. I came out on a real high.'

While we have focused on the extent to which the Place is Conducive to the proposed Process, the reverse must also be considered, especially where a time commitment is concerned.

A three-week residential programme may have been identified as the most appropriate Process for achieving the agreed Development Objectives. But if this amount of time spent away from work is not culturally acceptable or there are good business reasons that prevent it, then the Process is not Conducive to the Place. We find, for example, very few organisations who are comfortable to take the whole of the top management team off-site for an extended period however good the reason. Again there is a question mark against the extent to which there is a match between Process and Place.

Place to Performance Connection - Chance

This is the final Connection on the outside rim of the Model and returns to the Performance orientation above the Performance-Development Axis. The Critical Check question to be asked here is:

● Does the Place - ie the context - provide sufficient opportunities and possibilities for Performance attainment?

While in the previous section we were concerned with the impact of the environment on people's willingness or opportunity to develop, we are concerned here with the impact of the environment on the willingness or opportunity to perform.

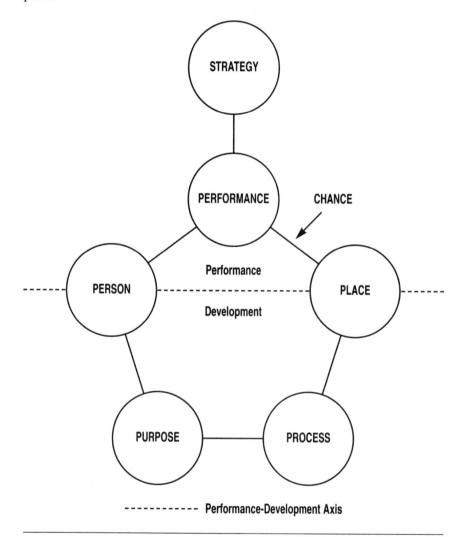

The Connection Check of Chance relates to whether, for example, there is sufficient time and opportunity to achieve the desired Performance. A very common failing in attempted changes to performance output is the lack of recognition given to the need for an individual manager both to deliver on his current job requirements, as well as developing to meet future job requirements. There are, unfortunately, only so many hours in the day!

Other issues within Chance that we encountered included:

- the realisation that one supervisor's team in a major manufacturing organisation was spread over a three-quarter-mile distance, yet he was supposed to monitor their work on a continuing basis (a bicycle was provided!)

- the lack of ready availability of pertinent and required information on a continuous basis (due to an inadequate IT system designed around hierarchical levels rather than performance processes)

- inappropriate rewards systems that either did not support the performance that was being demanded or, worse still, actively encouraged the wrong behaviour

- inappropriate 'role models' at the most senior levels in the organisation

Part of the Check on Chance may therefore be on the willingness and adaptability of managers to take the 'chance' of behaving in ways that are different from the influential role models, or which are not supported by the current systems and procedures. If, however, we are working actively to improve the effectiveness of our management development initiatives, we have to question whether we should be leaving these issues 'to chance'!

Snapshot

Knowing that the traditional hierarchical nature of the main manufacturing site tended to stifle ideas and entrepreneurialism, the CEO of a major engineering group set up his latest venture on a new site some 15 miles away. The leader of the new venture was an entrepreneur and created a culture within the new unit that actively encouraged the behaviour that was needed if the venture was to succeed.

Inner Connections or Cross-Braces

We have considered the series of Connection Checks that build necessary link-ages around the outside of the Wadenhoe Model, connecting each of the five Ps. However, these outer Connections are insufficient to provide for full integration of the Ps into a resilient and effective structure.

Engineers tell us that what we have now created is a mechanism rather than a structure, ie a structure that can flex and twist and potentially collapse in on itself. Further cross-bracing is necessary on the inside of the Model if it is to be self-supporting and resilient. A further five Connection Checks therefore need to be considered.

Performance to Purpose Connection - Contribution

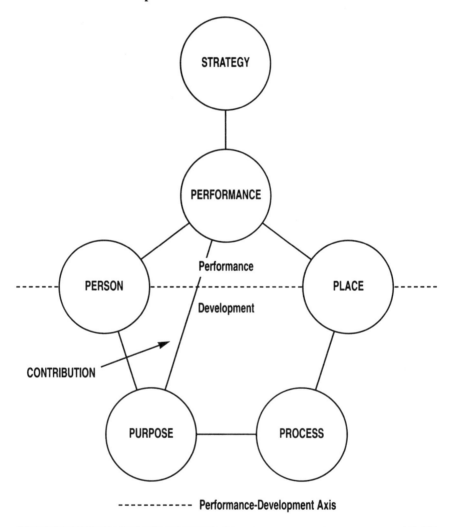

----------- Performance-Development Axis

The Critical Check question to be asked here is:

● Do the development objectives that have been defined for this group of managers correspond with their Performance objectives?

We have travelled around the outside of the Model in a process of translation where we have looked at the Competence Domains that are required and the perceived gaps in performance and have translated these into Competencies and Characteristics. In turn we have taken the perceived 'gap' in the Competencies and Characteristics and have translated these into Development Objectives.

The purpose of this Connection Check is to test whether the resultant Development Objectives recognisably Contribute to the managerial Performance required.

During the formation of The Model we were concerned that we had perhaps brought in an element of 'Chinese whispers' - maybe the original message had become totally lost in the number of steps that it had been through. We are therefore looking to ensure that we have not lost the sharp focus on the Performance needs of the organisation while travelling around our translation process. If we can test for Contribution, we are reassuring ourselves that the achievement of the Development Objectives that have been defined will deliver the performance results that we set out to achieve.

Snapshot
The inability of the top team to work effectively together was translated into a set of Development Objectives which focused on understanding teams and team roles. The Check for Contribution revealed that there had been a shift from skills development to knowledge-based objectives. The team 'knew' how to build teams - what they lacked were the skills to put their awareness into practise.

Performance to Process Connection - Credibility
The Critical Check question to be asked here is:

● Does the Development Process being planned have high perceived reality and relevance in relation to Performance?

One of the commonly heard comments on development programmes is 'What has this got to do with managing within my business?' This is a valid question where, for example, the participants are faced with the need to transform some

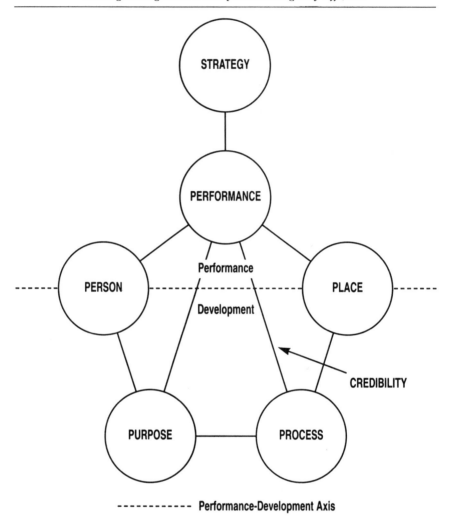

---------- **Performance-Development Axis**

generic concepts into the specific and relevant applications to their own jobs. Equally, they may be being asked, for example, to trust that the process of creating a personal collage from pictures cut from magazines will be contributing to their development in a key performance area.

This Connection Check therefore is concerned with the content and Process reality of the proposed Process and its Credibility in terms of the way that managers are being asked to Perform. This is not to say that every minute of every development process has to work exclusively within the reality of the manager's own organisation and position; but where participants are taken away from their reality it must be recognised and accepted that the Process should be designed to enable the necessary links to be made.

Snapshot

We use a case study written about 'Robin Hood' as a medium for introducing analyses for strategy formulation and implementation. Needless to say this is a long way from the reality of the managers who go through this Process. Without effective facilitation some managers would resist the idea that a medieval band of 'freedom fighters' had anything to say about managing in the final years of the twentieth century.

The facilitation that is required takes them step by step through the lessons in the case and how these might be applied back at work. Leaving the participants just to draw their own conclusion is rarely sufficient.

Person to Process Connection - Contracted

The Critical Check questions to be asked here are:

- Have the managers' own expectations about the Development Process been surfaced and acceptably accommodated into the Process design?

- Do the managers 'own' the Development Process in the sense of feeling committed to it?

- Have equitable and workable 'Contracts' about the Process been established?

Moving round the Model from the element of Performance to that of Person requires the 'gap' between the existing managerial Competencies and the Competencies that have been identified for managerial performance to be turned into Development Objectives.

Travelling further around the Model leads us to define the possible Development Processes that are likely to achieve the development. The purpose of the Person to Process Connection Check is to test that the selected Process is likely to be the most effective for this particular set of participants.

It also tests for the extent to which the participants understand the planned Process and feel committed to it. However senior the participants they will still have concerns and reservations about what they will be facing. The Contracted Check challenges whether these concerns and expectations have been suitably surfaced and dealt with.

One of the key issues is the preferred learning style of the participants, but there are others that also need to be considered in this 'Contracting' process. For example, before engaging in a Process participants will want to be convinced that the tutors have some knowledge and expertise that is relevant and acceptable to

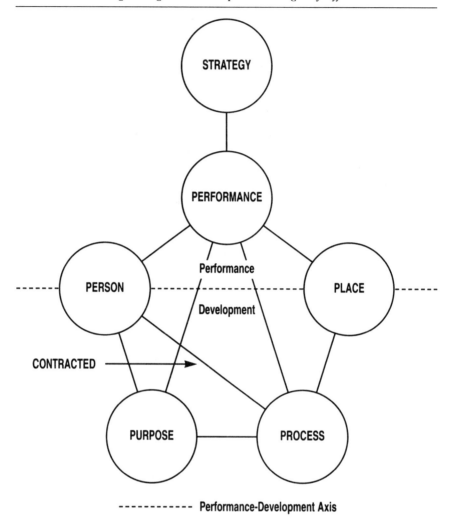

Performance-Development Axis

them. Thus the Check also tests for the sense of a shared commitment to the ideas, issues, values and goals that the Process plans to utilise.

The Contracted Check also relates for example to aspects of the length and intensity of the working day that has been defined in the Process. In attending a conference recently I was disappointed that in a day scheduled to run from 9.30 to 4.30 there were two hours of breaks. I did not feel that the Process represented value for my day. But equally, when the individuals expect time to socialise as part of the Process, they might find working after dinner unacceptable.

Finally, activity-based learning has become a significant process in our development armoury. Without adequate introduction and explanation as to its Purpose, it can be seen as 'playing games' and 'not what I have come for'.

This again is a key issue to be understood and agreed within the Contracted Check.

Snapshot

In working within a police force it was essential that we were seen to use first names when talking with the Chief Constable. This established us as having equal status with him, which in turn made us acceptable to the Chief Superintendents and other senior ranks.

Person to Place Connection - Concurrence

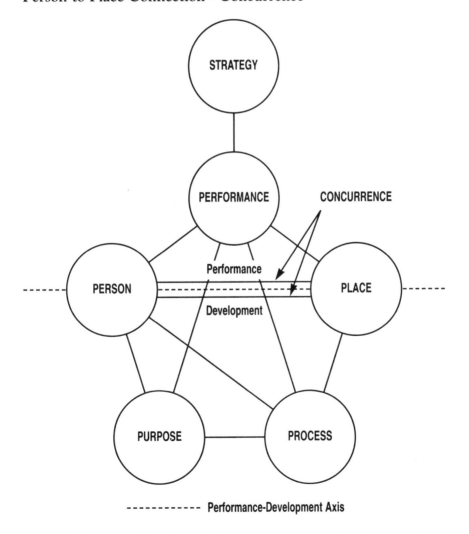

Performance-Development Axis

The Critical Check questions to be asked here are:

- Do the People and the Place match? For example, do the individual managers' values match those of the organisation culture?

- Do the managers' needs for power and control match the organisation's structure, etc?

For completeness we must see this as a double Connection, having implications both above and below the Performance-Development Axis. Above the Axis we are looking at the Concurrence between the individual and the operating environment; in an extreme, we are looking for the possibility of a square peg in a round hole, but more pragmatically we are looking for matching between the values and needs of the individual manager and the culture and style of the organisation. Without such a match it is unlikely that the individual manager will achieve the long-term performance that the organisation desires.

Below the Axis we are looking at the Concurrence between the values and needs of the individual and the ability of the organisation to provide an environment that encourages and supports their aspirations for development. The issue of Concurrence remains common, but we are looking at different aspects of both personality and culture in each case.

Many of the difficulties that are faced in organisations developing new strategic directions are concerned with the required shift in values for the organisation. Some individuals find a conflict between the declared values of the organisation and those that they hold themselves. The comment 'This is not what I joined for' is heard often around the National Health Service in the UK at the moment. Equally, managers may feel liberated by the revealed Concurrence between their deeply held beliefs and the new direction that the organisation is taking.

Snapshot

As the organisation moved towards empowered work teams the Manufacturing Director felt his need for control being steadily undermined. Eventually he had to leave to find an organisation where his style and values were more highly prized.

Below the Axis we see the individuals' expectation of being developed by the organisation year by year being challenged by the new competitive environment. They find themselves being placed in charge of their own development and feel let down by this apparent breach in their 'Psychological Contract'.

Snapshot

During the run-up to the creation of Trusts within the National Health Service a group of senior accountants, all of whom had some managerial responsibility, were discussing the changes. One said, 'I joined the NHS because I believed in its basic principles. Now all this is changing and I am powerless to do anything about it. I feel cheated.' There were nods of agreement from all except one of his colleagues, who significantly had only recently joined from industry.

Thus Concurrence can be both a liberating and empowering experience as well as being potentially threatening when it does not exist.

Purpose to Place Connection - Commissioned

The Critical Check questions to be asked here are:

● Do the Development Objectives carry weight in the organisation?

● Are they Championed with authority?

● Have the objectives been demanded, sanctioned and authorised?

As we have already seen, the element of Place has many components, and here we are considering Place in the Development arena. The feature of most importance here is the extent to which the senior management team and line managers of the managers whose development is being considered buy into the Development Objectives that have been identified.

Snapshot

The Executive responsible for Personnel had recognised for some time the need to change the way the company managed its resources. He had evidence that many of the key employees felt that their efforts were under-recognised and that there was too much of a gulf between the Executive of the company and the body of employees. Poor morale in some parts was reflected in sub-standard performance. Nominated managers were not managing or, more importantly, leading. He decided to institute a coaching skills course as a starting point to see if a change in managerial attitudes could be initiated. The series of courses started and appeared to be

Continued on next page

Continued from previous page

valued by most of the managers and supervisors who attended them, yet not much seemed to be changing in the workplace.

The tutors for the programme attended a meeting of the Executive Committee to report on progress. It came as a shock to the Executive responsible for Personnel that over half of the Committee denied their commitment to the programme. It was apparent that there was a tacit wish for the status quo to persist. This was less threatening to the Executive.

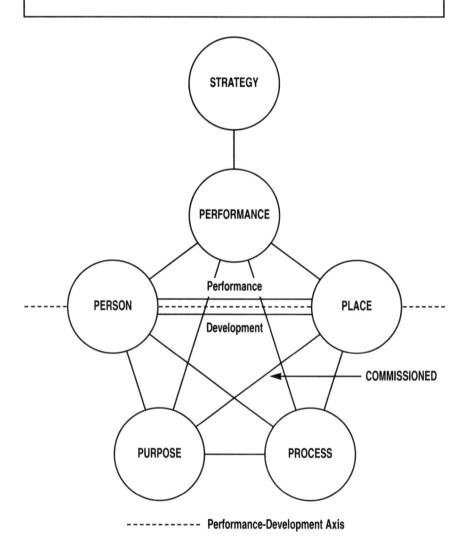

------------ Performance-Development Axis

Ownership of the Development Purpose as spelt out through objectives is at the heart of the issue. Do the key people feel that this is just another exercise that has originated from the personnel and training department or do they genuinely feel a sense of ownership of the Development actions? Do they feel that they have Commissioned the exercise in order to meet the performance needs? For the Development to be effective there must be a sense of it being demanded by line managers in the organisation rather than just being another routine.

The rigging is complete! - Summary

We now have a fully braced and resilient Model of strategically effective management development, which is Connected and integrated. While it remains flexible in so far as it can be used for any type of organisation, and entry can be made through different points, it is now robust enough to take the roughest of handling. This resilience has been achieved by working through each of the Connection Checks and building in the appropriate linkages between all the five Ps of the 5P Platform.

You should now understand the principles behind the Wadenhoe Model and the way that it can provide a framework for analysing the strengths and weaknesses of your organisation's approach to management development.

The next Chapter will start to look at the Analyses that exist to ensure that the Model is successfully launched into the working reality of your organisation.

Checklist for Chapter 6

Capability (Performance-Person Connection)

● Is there a match between Competencies (managers' ability to perform) and the Competence Domains (required performance areas)?

Contribution (Performance-Purpose Connection)

● Do managers' Development Objectives correspond to their Performance Objectives?

Credibility (Performance-Process Connection)

● Does the Development Process have high perceived reality and relevance in relation to Performance?

Chance (Performance-Place Connection)

- Does Place, ie the context, provide sufficient opportunities and possibilities for Performance attainment?

Concurrence (Person-Place Connection)

- Do the People and the Place match? For example, do the individual managers' values match those of the organisational culture? Do the managers' needs for power and control match the organisation's structures, etc?

Capacity (Person-Purpose Connection)

- Is there latent potential within the managers to develop further? What is their trainability? Do the Development Objectives match the targeted people?

Contracted (Person-Process Connection)

- Have the managers' expectations been surfaced and acceptably accommodated in the Process design? Do managers 'own' the Development Process? Have equitable and workable Contracts for development been established?

'Can do' (Purpose-Process Connection)

- Is the Process fit for the Purpose? Is there a reasonable probability that the Development Process can deliver its objectives (ie it is not 'pie in the sky')?

Commissioned (Purpose-Place Connection)

- Do the Development Objectives carry weight in the organisation? Are they Championed with authority? Have the objectives been demanded, sanctioned and authorised?

Conducive (Place-Process Connection)

- Is the Place Conducive to the Development Process? Is the context supportive of the Process?

Considering the Wadenhoe Model overall

- Is there **Congruence** between its elements?

● Is there **Consistency** across all its elements?

● Is the whole **Cohesive**, forming and providing a coordinated, mutually reinforcing, stable and yet flexible management development initiative?

● Is the initiative **Compatible** with other initiatives and adjacent sub-systems and Processes?

Chapter 7
'CHECKING FOR SEAWORTHINESS' - THE FIVE ANALYSIS STEPS

Introduction

At this stage in its development the Model should be well formed; its ingredients are assembled and have been checked for their Content. The Checks for Completeness have ensured that the Platform is appropriately balanced. With all the Connections in place and checked, the Model should be sturdy enough to withstand rugged use.

Putting the Model together has required considerable sifting and sorting of information, to the point where you might well ask whether 'paralysis by analysis' is a real danger. We believe that we have not yet reached that point. In fact, we have identified five steps for further analysis! These further Analyses may be seen as providing a Check for 'seaworthiness' of the Model before you launch it into the stormy seas of your organisation.

The five Analysis stages require you to check back on the work that you have done so far and to look at the bigger picture that you have been building up. It requires you to look at some of the broader interactions to ensure that you are still telling a meaningful story and that the parts continue to add up to the whole that you originally envisaged.

The various Analyses involve triangulation of three P elements at a time. These create summaries of the decisions that you have taken so far and are key to evaluating the rigour and the viability of your thinking in shaping the proposed management development interventions. Furthermore, they provide you with the opportunity to address issues that are exposed by the

Model, but which lie outside the traditional definition of management development.

The overall aim of this Chapter, therefore, is to carry out a 'sea trial' of the Model; in other words to carry out as many tests of the work that has been done so far as is possible without going 'live'.

By the end of the Chapter you should have rigorously inspected the Model, checked for any faults and remedied them. You should have confirmed in your own mind that the Model will work effectively when launched into the real world of your organisation.

The rest of this Chapter provides the details of the five Analysis stages. But before getting into these we need to introduce the concept of 'going off-line', since we shall refer to this as we progress each Analysis.

'Going off-line'

We have developed your understanding of the Wadenhoe Model as a dynamic tool that leads you towards improving the strategic effectiveness of your management development interventions. We have used it to identify the data that is needed to make decisions about development. But we also recognise that some of those decisions demand actions that are not generally regarded as within the scope of traditional management development activities.

For example, in looking at the Connection between Performance and Person we asked you to make the Critical Check on the Capability of the individual to perform in the way and to the standard that the organisation requires. Further, in looking to the Connection between Person and Purpose we asked you to make the Critical Check on the Capacity of the individual to develop further. What if the answer to both questions is 'No', ie that the individual's Competencies do not match the required performance areas and that the individual is unlikely to be trainable to these Competencies? What if you therefore conclude that there is a manager or a group of managers that you believe are never going to be capable of achieving the Performance that the Strategy of the organisation demands? What are you going to do about it?

The interventions generated by the Model are management development interventions. However, the Model will also highlight problems and issues requiring other actions within the broader scope of HR and even beyond that into decisions relating to the line and business management of the organisation. The need to go beyond management development to other solutions is what we refer to as 'going off-line'. In the examples above you may decide that the declared Strategy of the organisation is unachievable with the managers that you currently have. This might lead you to change aspects of the Strategy - or change the managers!

Either way, we are recognising that to continue blindly or naively in the belief that management development will resolve the problems is not an effective way forward.

Snapshot

An earlier snapshot featured managers who had neither the temperament nor the will to manage, but who would rather have stayed within their technical roles. An 'off-line' decision was made to remove the majority from managerial responsibility.

It could be asked whether this should have been checked before appointing them to managerial positions rather than being forced into the embarrassing 'off-line' position later. Social and other pressures may well have brought less than honest answers to any questions about willingness to perform in the roles. However, this selection process would have been more likely to have succeeded had the Competencies required for Performance in these roles been well-defined at the outset.

We will return to the idea of 'going off-line' as we consider each of the five Analysis stages.

Key Analysis Stages - the 5 As

The Analysis Stages require us to check back or to anticipate a bigger picture than we have considered so far. They require that we look at some of the larger interactions to check on the consistency of the story that we are telling and whether the parts add up to a meaningful whole. The Analyses involve triangulation of three P elements at a time as we evaluate the rigour and the viability of our decision-making in shaping the proposed management development interventions.

The five Analyses are:

1 Performance Potential Analysis

2 Development Needs Analysis

3 Development Place Analysis

4 Process Design Analysis

5 Cost Benefit Analysis

Performance Potential Analysis

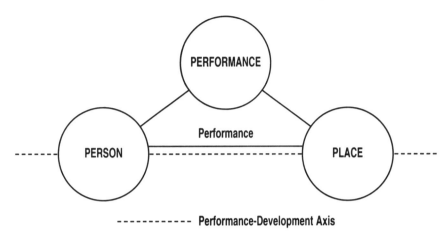

This Analysis asks the question:

● Is it possible for this Performance to be achieved by these People in this Place?

From an understanding of the Strategy of the organisation we can define the managerial Performance that is required for strategic success. We have used the Content Check to ensure that we have defined accurately the Competence Domains and that they are Central to strategic Performance achievement. We have also identified the Criteria or standards of Performance that are required. If this base of information and decision-making has not yet been established, we need to backtrack and plug these important gaps in the Model.

Similarly, we have checked the Content of Person in terms of the Competencies and Characteristics, Calibration and Communality. Again, we have considered Place in terms of the Content Checks of Culture, Confirmatory, Championed, Components and Convenient.

We have also checked the Connections between Person and Place (Concurrence), Performance and Place (Chance) and Person and Performance (Capability).

If the answer to the question 'Is it possible for this Performance to be achieved by these People in the Place?' remains 'No', even after we have revisited the Checks to look for errors, oversights or miscalculations, then we now need to consider the possibilities and need to 'go off-line'.

Thus, if on retracing your steps through the various Checks you still feel that your thinking is rigorous and correct but that there is still not the Performance Potential to deliver the organisation's Strategy, you may need to:

● 'Go off-line' from Performance. This might entail re-thinking the viability of the organisation's Strategy or even re-thinking the Strategy itself.

- 'Go off-line' from Person. This would involve us looking at aspects of our staffing, recruitment and selection policies and at the potential to replace the current cadre of managers.

- 'Go off-line' from Place. We may need, for example, to make changes to the facilities, resources, infrastructure and systems of the organisation where we recognise that they are actively disabling the desired Performance from being achieved.

Remembering the role of the Performance-Development Axis, we are looking at all these 'off-line' actions in the Performance arena.

'Going off-line' from Performance

Increasingly we see organisations where the HR function is actively involved in helping to develop the strategy. This obviously provides an opportunity to carry out some of the 'tempering' that may be required to ensure that the strategy is feasible in terms of the management and other people implications. In other organisations there is a separate process for creating an HR strategy that starts to work through the implications for people of the strategic direction.

If you have reached the conclusion that the Performance that is required for strategic success will not be delivered by the managers available, and that there are historic or cultural reasons why the managers cannot be replaced, then some rethinking of the strategy needs to take place. It may be possible to extend the time scales of the strategic objectives, or it may require the strategy to be fundamentally challenged.

As we have been through a process of defining managerial performance at the start of our use of the Wadenhoe Model, we may conclude that we have been too ambitious in these definitions. It may be possible to achieve the strategic aims of the organisation with lower Performance standards or by rearranging managerial responsibilities in a way that increases the potential for managers to perform.

As you can see, these actions are not within the traditional realms of management development. However, in our drive to make management development strategically effective we have to recognise that unless these issues are addressed we are potentially setting ourselves up to fail. It is not acceptable in the context of the Wadenhoe Model to go forward believing that the managers involved will not be able to achieve the desired level of Performance even after development.

> **Snapshot**
>
> We sat down with the Personnel Director of a major organisation to try and extract an implied strategy from the actions and comments of the highly autocratic Chief Executive. By using the Model to understand the Performance Potential implications of this strategy and thus realising the impossibility of what was apparently intended, the Personnel Director was able to influence the shape of the strategy through his interactions with the Chief Executive in a way that enabled the existing management cadre to perform.

'Going off-line' from Person

If it is accepted that the strategy of the organisation is indisputable, the second 'off-line' action leads us to look at the individual or individuals involved. In the short term we may decide that it is possible to move or replace the managers concerned. This may involve retirement or an active process to help the individual find an alternative role elsewhere.

> **Snapshot**
>
> One of the major consultancies has an active policy of managing people through the organisation. Rather than promote people into a Partnership role that they are incapable of fulfilling or unsuitable to fulfil, they work with the individual to find a more suitable role in another organisation. This is a recognised and accepted method for managing performance.

In the long term there may be a need to modify the organisation's policies of recruitment and selection to ensure that as vacancies occur they are filled by people who do have the potential to achieve the Performance that is required.

'Going off-line' from Place

We have commented earlier about the strength of the influence that the Place has on management development effectiveness. If the conclusion is that there are aspects of the environment that are having an adverse effect on the Performance of individuals, work must be carried out to change them.

These may be aspects of the systems, structure or style of the organisation. Often, for example, we have seen organisation cultures with a strong 'fear' element, which works against the risk-taking behaviour that the strategy demands.

To ignore these factors or to hope that someone else will recognise the problem and deal with them is not likely to increase the strategic impact of our management development interventions. If we are to make management development strategically effective we again need to go 'off-line' from the Model and work on these issues.

Snapshot

In a major insurance group the strategy required the development of larger accounts. Yet the departmental finance structure actively encouraged the development of many small accounts. Until the funding system was changed there was little incentive for anyone to perform in the way that the strategy required.

In the spirit of making management development strategically effective you can see how the Performance Potential Analysis is highlighting issues that have a material impact on the effectiveness of our management development interventions. In addition it is leading us to address those issues by working in areas that are beyond the traditional management development boundaries. Yet without actively addressing these issues we are potentially setting expectations for managerial change that no development programme can deliver.

Development Needs Analysis

This Analysis asks the question:

● Is this the appropriate Development to enable this Person (or these People) to achieve this Performance?

This Analysis spans across the Performance-Development Axis in joining together the elements of Performance, Person and Purpose.

We have by now used the Content Check to ensure that we have defined accurately the Competence Domains and that they are Central to strategic Performance achievement. We have also identified the Criteria or standards of Performance required. As we discussed in the first Analysis stage above we have Checked the Content of Person in terms of Competencies and Characteristics, Calibration and Communality.

We should also have Checked on the Content of Purpose by looking at the 'Causes' or Development Objectives, their Criticality and their Currency.

We will also have worked on the Connection Checks between Performance and Person (Capability), between Person and Purpose (Capacity) and between Purpose and Performance (Contribution).

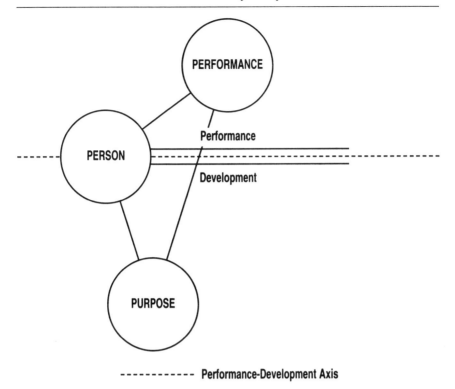

------------ **Performance-Development Axis**

If the answer to our question 'Is this the appropriate Development to enable this Person (or these People) to achieve this Performance?' is 'No', we will have to revisit these previous Checks to look for possible errors or oversights.

If we still conclude that the work and the thinking that we have carried out is rigorous and accurate, we are drawn again to the need to 'go off-line'. Thus on determining that this is not the appropriate Development to enable these People to Perform we may need to:

● 'Go off-line' from Performance. If we are working steadily through the steps of Analysis, we have considered this need already in terms of thinking about the viability of the declared strategy.

● 'Go off-line' from Person. Again, we should by now have considered the need to replace people in the short or long term with others who are likely to be able to Perform in the required manner. As we are also looking at aspects of Person below the Performance-Development Axis our consideration will also entail aspects of recruitment and selection that relate to the development capacity of the individual.

● 'Go off-line' from Purpose. Here the need is to challenge the curricula that have been developed in response to the declared Development Objectives.

In the first Analysis we considered the three off-line areas that were exposed, ie 'going off-line' from Performance, Person and Place. We have already looked therefore at the need to review the strategic aims of the organisation in the light of their implications for managerial performance and where necessary to modify those strategic aims.

Similarly, in looking at the element of Person we considered the need in the short or long term to replace the current managers who are identified as being incapable of performing in the required manner with others who can. As we are crossing over the Performance-Development Axis in this Analysis we may also need to consider replacing managers in the short or long term who lack the capacity to develop to the desired performance standards.

'Going off-line' from Purpose

The 'off-line' action that we have not yet considered is the need to 'go off-line' from Purpose. If we believe that this is not the appropriate Development to enable the managers involved to achieve the desired performance, we may need to look at the content or curricula that have been identified for any development activity.

Have we, for example, lost sight of the overall aims of any development activity and arrived at a set of Development Objectives that are of value to the individual but which are not going to contribute to the managerial Performance that was the original intent? Have we followed slavishly an outside curriculum, eg an IPM course or MBA programme, that is not appropriate for the needs of our organisation?

Snapshot

The Chief Engineer of an engineering group was sent on a Public General Management Programme that focused on interpersonal skills. He was mystified as to why he had been sent. 'I am the Chief Engineer; I have no one reporting in to me and I have made it quite clear that I do not want the responsibility for other people. If they try to make me head the department I shall leave.'

Losing this focus will take us 'off-line' to track down the weakness in the data that has enabled us to develop the wrong objectives. Have we selected the wrong Competencies or placed the wrong emphasis on their improvement? Have we fudged our judgement of Capability or Capacity and are now being forced to recognise that the individual will not be able to achieve the Performance that is required whatever the development effort?

Snapshot

Having identified that the strategy required the Board of Directors of an engineering group to work more effectively together, a team-building course was developed. While the participants enjoyed the programme and agreed that it would be valuable to them in developing their departmental teams, it was also recognised that the issues within the Board were caused by clashes of personality rather than the lack of team-building skills. A subsequent workshop was developed around a personality profiling tool and achieved the desired breakthrough in behaviour.

Development Place Analysis

The third of our five Analysis stages looks at the elements of Person, Place and Purpose. In this Analysis we are considering all three of these elements below the Performance-Development Axis. This Analysis asks the question:

● Is this Development for this Person (or these People) possible in this Place?

From our earlier work we will now have Checked the Content of Person above

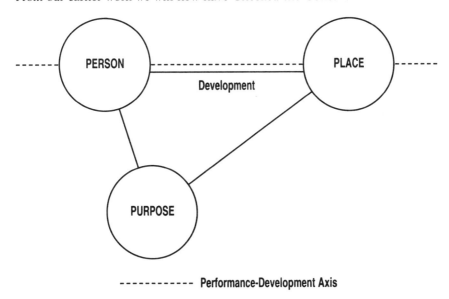

and below the Performance-Development Axis in terms of Competencies and Characteristics, Calibration and Communality. We have considered Place above and below the Axis in terms of the Content Checks of Culture, Confirmatory, Championed, Components and Convenient. In addition, we have carried out the Content Checks on Purpose for 'Causes' or Development Objectives, Criticality and Currency.

We have travelled along the Connection Checks between Person and Purpose that we called Capacity and checked whether there was a latent potential for the individual to develop further. We travelled the Connection between Purpose and Place checking the extent to which the Development Objectives were Commissioned appropriately in the organisation. Finally, we have checked along the Connection between Place and Person for a sense of Concurrence.

As with the other Analyses that we have carried out we are now testing the 'seaworthiness' of our thinking so far, before we launch into development activities. So what happens if the answer to our Analysis question is 'No'? What do we do if having worked around the Model in a rigorous and logical way we are forced to conclude that it is not possible for this Development to be achieved by this Person in this Place?

Again the answer may be to go 'off-line'. We will assume that by now you will have rechecked your work on the elements, their Content and Connections. So the possibilities are to:

- 'Go off-line' from Person. We have now considered the implication of this both above and below the Performance-Development Axis.

- 'Go off-line' from Purpose. In the Analysis above we considered the need to look again at the content and curricula of the proposed intervention.

- 'Go off-line' from Place. We have looked at the need to go off-line from Place above the Performance-Development Axis and we now need to look at the implications below the Axis.

'Going off-line' from Place below the Performance-Development Axis

Our considerations of Place have included both the workplace and the venue for any formal development event. Attention is often given to certain aspects of the venue for any development activity - especially the leisure facilities! However, the more serious concern is whether it is an environment in which the individual can achieve the desired development. We are often asked whether there will be feedback from the development event to the participants' senior managers: 'Is this a safe environment in which I can experiment, make a fool of myself, but learn without worrying whether my every move is being watched and reported on?'

Snapshot

The senior tutor at a UK business school based in a magnificent country house greets the junior managers who arrive by minibus at the start of a three-week general management programme. 'Many of them are terrified when they see the place. Despite the joining instructions about dress and informality they are totally overawed by the building. It takes me several days to relax them to the point where the learning is starting to take place.'

I am sure that we are all equally aware of the reverse situation where senior managers cannot relax in an environment where they are worried about whether vital messages will get through or where the accommodation is unappealing.

However, as we identified earlier our chief focus is on the workplace as an environment for development. Will people be allowed sufficient time and opportunity to experiment and thereby develop? What is the organisation's attitude to failure? If the culture tends to punish failure, some work needs to be done to try and provide a mentored environment in which, for example, the individual is shielded.

Snapshot

Participants on a two-year part-time MBA programme were reflecting on the difficulties of holding down a full-time job while pursuing a demanding degree programme. Most felt that their employers had been very generous and understanding during the first year, but by the second year they had tended to forget the time needed to attend the course and were irritated by the participants' lack of availability for critical meetings.

As we have considered in the two previous Analyses, it may be necessary to carry out remedial work on some of these issues 'off-line' in order to increase the likely impact of the planned management development intervention.

Process Design Analysis

This Analysis works in two parts. In the first it links together the three elements of Person, Purpose and Process and asks the question:

● Is this the right Process to achieve this Development for this Person (or these People)?

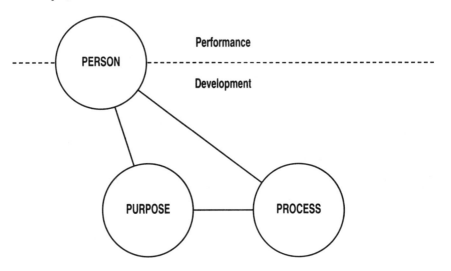

In the second part it links the elements of Person, Process and Place and asks the question:

● Is this the right Process for this Person (or these People) in this Place?

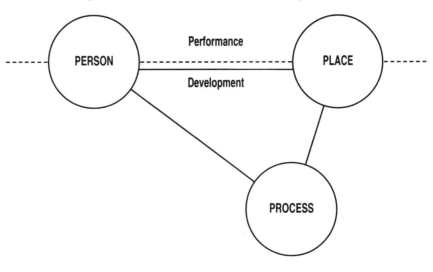

In each of these Analyses we are working below the Performance-Development Axis, ie we are in the Development Arena.

As before, we assume that you have worked with rigour and integrity through the Checks of Content, Completeness and Connection. You will have looked at each of the elements both individually and in pairs as part of the Connection Checks. This final stage before taking the Model 'live' requires you to lift your sights to cover these elements to ensure that the bigger picture still holds true and that you have not been side-tracked by any of the inevitable detail.

Similarly, our concern is when the answer to either of the Analysis questions is 'No'. The first reaction will of course be to return to the Checks for Content and Connection to see whether anything has escaped our thinking; to look for errors or miscalculations.

If there are none, and we have already looked at the 'off-line' implications of the elements of Person, Purpose and Place, our remaining 'off-line' possibility is to look at Process.

'Going off-line' from Process

Snapshot

The training officer had determined that the managers working in the finance function throughout the organisation needed to be developed into a more effective team. A training provider was identified who made extensive use of the outdoors as the Process. The managers were informed of the dates and were 'committed to the development'. A chance visit by the provider revealed that one of the participants had a broken leg, two had severe arthritis and one was recovering from recent open-heart surgery!

At one level we would have expected such an extreme case as this to be picked up during the Connection Check between Person and Process of Contracting. How could these individuals have agreed to this Process knowing their physical limitations? It transpired that none of them had experienced any form of development and were entirely ignorant of the implications of what they were embarking on. In addition the training officer was a strong disciple of this form of development.

Thus, the 'off-line' action here is to investigate alternative methods of development that would be more appropriate for these people.

In the second part of the Process Design Analysis we are concerned with the suitability of the Process in relation to both the Purpose and the Place. By way of illustrating the issues, action learning has achieved a revival in recent years as organisations have been attracted by the 'real' nature of the Process. However, it gives rise to the question of whether the organisation has sufficient 'real' projects for the participants to work on. Does the culture encourage people to learn 'on the job'? Are there sufficient mentors in the organisation who will 'own' the projects in a way that facilitates the desired learning?

Snapshot

A group of senior managers who had attended a management development programme wanted to set themselves up as a task force when they returned to work in order both to offer their new skills to the organisation at large and also to continue with their own development. The culture of the organisation was highly task focused and anyone with 'time to take on something extra' was viewed with suspicion. Even though they proposed working in their own time they had to drop the idea.

Here the 'off-line' work that may be necessary could be to focus the task force on tasks that are perceived by the organisation as 'real', ie they need to be done. This might remove the image of the task force indulging their spare time. Alternatively, it might be possible to identify a more culturally acceptable way of integrating their learning back into the organisation. In either case there is 'off-line' work to be carried out on the Process.

Cost Benefit Analysis

The fifth of our Analyses is both the most obvious and the most difficult. It links together the elements of Performance and Purpose with the Strategy of the organisation. The question is, however, relatively simple.

● If the Development Objectives are achieved will the contribution to enhanced Performance be worth the cost when set against the Strategic progress? Will the management development initiative be of sufficient consequence to justify proceeding?

The overall aim of our management development initiatives is to impact positively on the strategic performance of the organisation. It is a fair question to ask therefore, 'If your managers were performing in the way that you have defined what impact would it have on the long-term performance of the organisation?'

Snapshot
In asking this question of a client recently I was told 'A minimum of 10 per cent on the bottom line - £3 million per annum'. The potential benefits of strategically effective management development can be significant!

Yet this is a question that is asked only infrequently, and then only rarely answered. If it is answered the reply is most often highly subjective. We know that the ideal for anyone in management development is to make an unambiguous causal link between management development activities and the bottom-line performance of the organisation. As we get more proficient at handling the other

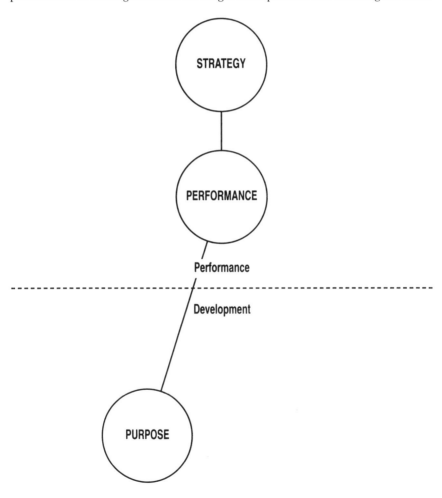

STRATEGY

PERFORMANCE

Performance

- -

Development

PURPOSE

forms of evaluation the ideal becomes more tantalising. (See Chapter 10 for our response to this need.) However, if our answer to the challenge of the contribution that the enhanced managerial performance is making to the strategic aims is inconclusive, perhaps we should be reconsidering the initiative.

Certainly, we may need to re-examine the link between the Strategy and managerial Performance. This is the link that we call **Consequence**. What is the Consequence of the Performance? What is the Consequence of managers not performing in the manner and to the standard that is required?

If we are concerned that the costs of the initiative outweigh the potential benefits, there may be a need for 'off-line' work at either end of this chain. Are the strategic aims sufficiently demanding or is there a need to re-examine the Strategy of the organisation. Remember in the first Analysis we considered whether the Strategy was too demanding on People. Here we need to decide whether the Strategy is demanding enough!

At the other end of the scale, are we embarking on a development programme that is simply too ambitious and costly for the returns that it will deliver?

Conclusions

In the previous Chapters we have looked at the elements that go to make up the Wadenhoe Model. We have checked the Platform for Completeness; we have Checked each of the elements for Content; and we have checked the nature and the strength of the Connections that give the Model its stability. We still have to examine in the next Chapter the way in which the maturing Model is courted and subsequently married into the organisation, and the actions that are required to maintain the potency of the Model so as to avoid premature divorce (!). But here we have been doing the fitness tests and checks on the total structural integrity of the Model in anticipation of taking such steps towards implementation.

The five Analyses have linked together three of the elements at a time in a triangulation of the outcomes. They have forced us to re-examine, where appropriate, decisions and thinking that we have already worked through to ensure that there are no gaps or oversights.

But most importantly the Analysis stages have firmly re-established our management development thinking within the organisation. They have recognised that management development and management performance do not take place in isolation, and that if we are to be effective in making management development a key strategic tool we have to take responsibility for actively managing issues that have a direct impact on our interventions.

Thus, the concept of 'going off-line' has taken us out of the traditional arenas of management development. It has highlighted the need to be active in other aspects of the organisation that will impact on the strategic effectiveness of our management development initiatives.

The Model has been thoroughly tested and appears sound. In the next Chapter we will consider what is necessary for the successful introduction, implementation, maintenance and refinement of a management development strategy and the initiatives that it includes.

We said at the outset of this book that we see the Wadenhoe Model as a key strategic tool. For it to remain valuable we need to also look at how it will be maintained in the organisation. These are the Checks for Construction and Carrying-Out.

In the final Chapter we will return to the theme of 'Putting a Measure on Management Development'.

Checklist for Chapter 7

Performance Potential Analysis

● Is it possible for this Performance to be achieved by this Person/these People in this Place?

Development Needs Analysis

● Is this the appropriate Development to enable this Person/these People to achieve this Performance?

Development Place Analysis

● Is it possible for this Development to be achieved by this Person/these People in this Place?

Process Design Analysis

● Is this the right Process to achieve this Development for this Person/these People?

● Is this the right Process for this Person/these People in this Place?

Cost Benefit Analysis

● If the Development Objectives are achieved, will the contribution to enhanced managerial Performance be worth the cost when set against the Strategic progress?

● Will the management development initiative be of sufficient consequence to justify proceeding?

Chapter 8
'LAUNCHING THE INITIATIVE' - PLATFORM CONSTRUCTION AND CARRYING-OUT CHECKS

Introduction

In developing the Wadenhoe Model we would have liked, of course, to create a Model that was simultaneously

- **Generaliseable** across a range of organisations

- **Simple** to understand by organisation members

- **Accurate** in its application within an organisation.

However, as we indicated in an earlier Chapter in the real world it is only ever possible for a Model to possess two out of these three characteristics at the same time. We have developed a Model that is **Generaliseable** and (relatively) **Simple**. At best then it must be an approximation to the 'truth', ie the reality within a particular organisation.

The implication of this status of the Model is that it requires you, the user, to supply the **Accuracy**, and in so doing to produce a Model that is specific to your organisation - sacrificing Generaliseability but enabling the achievements of Simplicity and Accuracy. This is where the step-by-step rigour of the Model comes in. We intend that you should supply the Accuracy to the Model by interpreting and applying the concepts in the specific realities of your organisation, and we have supplied you with a process of Checks and Analyses for doing this.

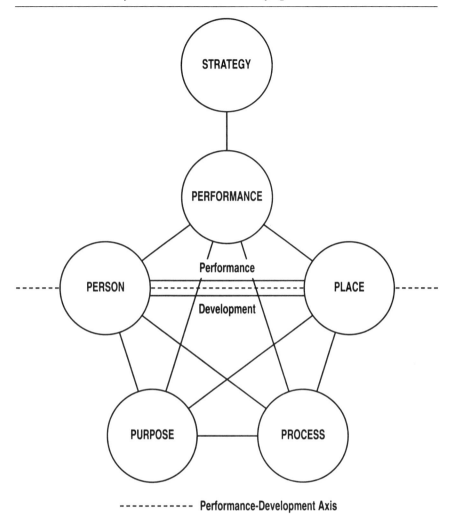

------------ **Performance-Development Axis**

At the same time we believe that the Model is Simple to understand in concept. We hope that the easily memorable labelling of the five Ps for the Platform, the five Cs for the Critical Checks and the five Analysis stages to give the Model the 'once over' will aid your understanding.

However, that in itself is not enough. Not only you but others in the organisation need to understand the Model and its features and to see its relevance and advantages. All our experience indicates that for a management development initiative to be successfully launched, people other than just its designers need to comprehend it and be committed to it. All too often such comprehension and commitment is sought only after the intervention has been designed and constructed (if it is ever sought at all!).

Snapshot

The newly appointed HR manager of a large company found a considerable amount of money being spent on management training activities. He could see no links between this and the strategic needs of the organisation. He therefore cancelled all management development activities until the senior Executives of the organisation had been through a development programme of their own to identify development needs. Only when the Executives had completed this programme and were able to see and understand the links between the development activities and the strategy of the organisation were the management development activities reinstated.

This Chapter sets out five Construction Checks, which help to ensure that in assembling the Model you do so in a way that predicates for a successful launch.

Having worked through the Model in the way that we have been proposing we believe that you will have created a management development initiative that will contribute positively to the strategic aims of your organisation. But we have one last outstanding concern. We have developed the concept of the Wadenhoe Model not as a one-off process but as a way of continuing to maintain the strategic effectiveness of your management development initiatives.

The world in which we operate and compete continues to increase in complexity. Change is no longer an intermittent event but an everyday fact of life, and we see little sign of these turbulent conditions changing in the near future. The Model gives us our best shot at dealing with the situation as we currently see it. But it will need to be adapted, updated, refined, monitored and evaluated if it is to retain its power to influence the organisation. We need to be continually learning about the performance and development of managers in our organisation, and to use this learning as we go along and to plan for the next initiative. Hence, the final of our set of five C Checks - the Carrying-Out Checks.

Snapshot

'We have been running this three-week programme for middle managers for five years now. Everyone enjoys it and it has become part of the reward for being promoted - people look forward to it. I don't really know what value we gain from it, but if I try to stop it I will be prevented by all the senior managers who went through the same programme.'

In this Chapter we will look in detail at the Construction and Carrying-Out Checks. By the end of the Chapter you should have:

● Ensured that the process of identifying and assembling the Model has been carried out in a manner that predicates for a successful launch

● Understood and put in place the necessary activities for maintaining and modifying the Model in implementation.

Platform Construction Check

The overall question that we are examining here is:

● Has the process of identifying and assembling the Model been carried out in a manner that predicates for a successful launch?

The Critical Checks on Construction are:

Consultation
Has opinion in the organisation been canvassed and involvement sought? Has consultation taken place and a coalition established with the interested parties and stakeholders in this initiative?

Communication
Has information been honestly exchanged on the key issues? Have intentions been clearly conveyed, actions explained and rationales provided?

Consideration
Have the concerns of managers been surfaced and acknowledged, for example their hopes, fears, needs and aspirations? Have the benefits and personal pay-offs been identified?

. . .in order to achieve:

Comprehension
Is there an understanding amongst managers of the overall situation and an understanding in terms of their personal implications?

Commitment
Is there a willingness, desire and drive amongst managers for Development and Performance achievement?

Let us look at the implications of each of these in turn.

Consultation

As you have gone through this book we hope that you will have sought out the information that is required to hold the Model up against your own organisation. Though it may not be fully recognised, seeking information of this kind is part of the Consultation process, and this questioning is also a development intervention in its own right. For example, by asking the Directors to be clear about the Strategy of the organisation and therefore to determine the Performance implications you are likely to have influenced strongly the thinking inside the organisation. It is also ground that can prove to be challenging, since such questions can be confronting and exposing to those who are responsible for strategic thinking in the organisation.

But within this Check we are asking you to go a stage further. In the earlier Connection Check 'Commissioned' we asked you to identify the key individuals inside the organisation whose backing to this new rigorous approach to development was needed if it was to become 'the way that we do management development around here'.

Here we are asking you to throw the net wider to include all parties who are likely to be affected by or interested in the actions that are being proposed, and to canvass their opinions. For example, we clearly need line managers to improve the quality of their Performance review processes so that there is a steadily increasing quality of objective information available to us. Have they been included in the Consultation process, and do they feel involved in what you are proposing? Do they understand and value the comprehensive approach that you are undertaking with the Model and the benefits that it is intended to bring to the organisation? Who else needs to be included in the thinking process?

Snapshot

In introducing a senior management development programme into an organisation it was decided to ask the secretaries and PAs of these people to go through the proposed programme first. It was felt that if they understood what was involved they were more likely to encourage their bosses to attend and to make space in their diaries.

Communication

While the process of Consultation is an essential and obvious step in this process, it should not be confused with the sharing and discursive nature of Communication. Any form of management development involves change. We know from recent research into the experiencing of change by managers just how vital is the need for effective Communication before, during and after the event. There is a need for people to understand fully the integrity that lies behind the decisions and to feel that they have been given an opportunity to discuss and challenge them.

Thus, the emphasis here is on the provision of a rationale for what is happening, and on the need, where possible, to be open and honest about your intentions and actions.

Similarly, there is a need for clarity and a shared understanding of what is planned, what it is intended to achieve, and the impact that it is likely to have if the initiative is not to be severely hindered during implementation.

Snapshot

On a recent development workshop one of the participants sat with me at lunch. 'I was just told to come on this workshop with an open mind. I really did not want to come - I thought it would expose me. So my mind was open, but only just! If only someone had really talked it through with me before I came I could have got so much more out of the experience. Why did they not feel able to tell me honestly what they wanted me to gain from the programme?'

It is becoming widely recognised that we rarely have time in our organisations for 'conversations' - the free-flowing exchange of ideas and values out of which a true understanding can develop. We hold meetings and chair discussion groups, but their very process can be inhibiting with their formal agendas and tight time scales. To be effective the process we are identifying here requires a quality conversation.

Consideration

In a recent discussion with a group of senior managers it was felt that many change initiatives failed to take account of and respond to where individuals were 'at', and failed to translate and redefine the initiative in personal terms by acknowledging the natural anxieties and pressures on the managers concerned. The managers felt that there was a greater need to talk about the benefits for the individual rather than solely the benefits to the organisation.

The question that we are raising here therefore concerns the extent to which the concerns of managers have been surfaced and acknowledged. Have the benefits and the personal pay-offs of the planned development activity been identified? Do we fully understand the nature of the hopes and aspirations, fears and concerns, that are being voiced? Are we sure that we have even gathered the full extent of the concerns that individuals may feel?

Snapshot

Throughout the development programme a manager had been remote and withdrawn - at times downright surly. This was behaviour that was quite out of character. It was only towards the end of the three days that he revealed that his three-month-old twins were going through some important medical tests that week and he was very concerned. But in the culture of that organisation one did not express personal feelings and therefore his concerns had not been taken account of when deciding on his attendance on the programme.

We have identified throughout this book that development involves taking risks. It involves doing things that might not work at first, and learning from the experience. It is an obvious point to make that we each will need to feel that there is some benefit to be gained from taking the risk. Has the nature of the benefit to the individual been explored? In many organisations now there is an understandable reluctance to promise promotion and progression as a result of attending a development programme. But what does the individual have to gain by going through the process, and is the potential gain sufficient to make the risk worthwhile? And has this been discussed and explored with the individual?

The aim of the first three elements of this Construction Check, ie Consultation, Communication and Consideration, is to provide an effective base for the final two Checks for Comprehension and Commitment, without which the initiative has a poor chance of success.

Comprehension

The issue within the Check on Comprehension is the extent to which the individual understands both the big picture of organisational performance and development and the smaller picture of individual implications.

Do the individuals understand the context in which a change in their Performance is required? The organisation has been successful in the past, so why do things need to change now? Do individuals understand the strategic intentions of the organisation in a way that affects the way that they behave? Or is the strategy seen as an annual exercise to keep the shareholders happy, but which has little or no impact on what really happens?

If they do understand the strategic intentions of the organisation, do they make the necessary link with their own performance? 'Yes, the organisation is going through a total quality exercise, but why do I have to behave differently?'

'I have always behaved in this way - they must appreciate that because they have always given me a high appraisal rating and promoted me.'

Snapshot

In the middle of a major Business Process Re-engineering exercise the accountant asked to see the Managing Director. In the new organisation he was being asked to be a financial consultant to the emerging process teams. 'I have been in the profession for thirty years and I am only now starting to understand accountancy. It is a really useful tool that people out there need and value. I wish I had understood this years ago.'

We should not be surprised or dismayed by this apparent lack of Comprehension. The nature of many of our organisations has developed compliant and dependent cultures that have discouraged the challenging Comprehension that is required here. However, although it may be self-evident, we should never lose sight of the fact that managers need to understand things in order to be effective in them.

Commitment

The final Check in the Platform Construction is to consider whether managers in the organisation feel a sufficient and real Commitment to improving managerial Performance and to using effective management development as the tool to achieve this. Do managers believe that the organisation's strategic competitive advantage will depend upon the quality of its people? Do managers value the role of management development in helping them to improve their own performance and the performance of their direct reports?

More specifically, do the managers involved in the specific initiative, including the participants, mentors, etc, feel a sense of Commitment to the initiative?

We have asked in the previous Check whether the managers Comprehend what is being proposed. But Comprehension is not enough. For management development to be effective we need the managers to be totally sold on the idea and to feel an emotional Commitment to carrying it through with a full understanding of the consequences. Without their will and desire we are left with the traditional approach of imposing the development, of coercing the performance improvement and of demanding change.

There is evidence enough of the impact of a fully motivated Commitment as opposed to compliant acceptance. The Check here is to understand the extent and the nature of the real Commitment that exists.

Conclusion

Over the years much has been written comparing Western and Eastern business approaches, particularly the difference in approaches to changes in management style and processes and the introduction of new ideas and products. Emphasis has been placed on the extensive process of consultation and involvement that takes place in Japan, for example, to avoid problems prior to implementation - to avoid resistance rather than having to deal with it. It is also recognised that this process enables more people to contribute to the chosen solution, often resulting in better quality thinking and ideas.

We see the same lessons to be learned in management development. The Construction Checks are designed to ensure as much as possible that any potential objections to the idea or flaws in the thinking are exposed at the outset while there is still time to make changes.

Platform Carrying-Out Checks

We have emphasised all along the role of the Wadenhoe Model as an organiser for our thoughts. It is not a disposable Model to be used once, then discarded. However, if it is to continue to be relevant and valuable within the fast-moving environment in which most businesses operate, it needs to be maintained, updated, refined and modified in the light of experience and changing circumstances.

The aim of the Carrying-Out Checks is to ensure that the necessary activities are in place for maintaining and modifying the Model during the implementation of the selected intervention.

We need to be continually learning about the performance and development of managers. We need to monitor and evaluate the results of using the Model and modify our approach in the light of this learning. We need to monitor constantly the nature of managerial performance in the light of the changes in the strategy of the organisation.

In the past it was legitimate to expect the strategic plan of the organisation to have a 'shelf life' of a number of years. Now we are more comfortable with the notion of 'emergent planning', ie strategies that follow broadly agreed tracks, but which flex and respond to competitor and customer trends as they emerge. Our approach to management development must be similar. We have to expect that the needs and the solutions that have emerged this year will be replaced by other needs next year. This is not to say that we got it wrong this year! It is simply the rate at which the demands on managers are changing.

Equally, however, we are not advocating a 'flavour of the month'/'butterfly' approach to management development. More than enough money has been wasted on initiatives that were introduced with little or no thought given to their implications. The 'quick fix', the latest good idea and the narrow solution are anathema to the Wadenhoe Model, and are, we believe, some of the major reasons for the low impact of management development initiatives.

Instead, the Carrying-Out Checks emphasise perseverance, consistency, monitoring, checking, learning, adapting, capturing, improving, recording and, having got there, evaluating and producing further learning for next time!

The Checks that we are proposing for Platform Carrying-Out are therefore as follows:

Continuity

Will people persevere with the approach? Will there be a Continuity of effort? Will momentum be maintained and the steer held?

Checking

Have systems been devised and responsibilities agreed for monitoring, controlling and maintaining the initiative? Have communication channels been opened to enable on-going dialogue and feedback? Will there be a constant checking of 'our course'?

Capturing learning

Has an action learning orientation been instilled? Have the processes and skills for critical reflection and learning from experience been developed and adopted?

Changing

Is the 'development model' that is being adopted open and amenable to change in response to altered circumstances? While maintaining a resilience in the face of obstacles, is the approach flexible and capable of being modified in accord with developments? Are the means in place for making and holding/consolidating improvements on a continuous basis?

Chronicling

Have mechanisms been set up for the chronicling of events, the keeping of records, the collection of data for logistics and evaluation purposes? Is there a record of the resources used, the participants' reactions, the learning and the outcomes?

Continuity

> ## Snapshot
>
> The Board of a major engineering group expressed their total commitment to the planned senior managers programme. It was recognised that the organisation needed a Critical Mass to go through the programme quickly if the required change was to be achieved. The first group of managers went through the programme to critical acclaim. However, an upturn in the business meant that managers were now too busy to attend and all further programmes were postponed.

It was accepted that the programme was required and the desired Performance change was happening, but when other pressures emerged there was no will to maintain the Continuity and to persevere with the initiative.

The Check that we are proposing here is to ensure as far as possible that the agreed development programme will be pursued as long as it is delivering the agreed benefits to the organisation.

Checking

As defined, Checking is about monitoring and controlling, keeping in touch with and progressing the planned Process. Have communication channels been established to enable us to collect feedback from participants and their managers?

> ## Snapshot
>
> In his opening remarks at the start of each senior managers' programme the Chief Constable made sure that every participant was given his home phone number. 'I expect to hear from you about the programme and whether we have got it right. If you don't call me, I will be calling you.'

Capturing learning

To remind ourselves, the Checks in this section are concerned with the implementation of the Model. We are checking here therefore on the ways in which we will learn about the Model in implementation. Are we capturing the learning about the Model in a way that will enable us to modify or update the Model in the light of changing circumstances? We have recognised that some of our planning will be 'emergent', and the Model needs to respond to this.

Snapshot

A formal part of the timetable of each programme was the time that the management development team sat down to discuss the progress in implementation of the Model. This took place two weeks after the event to allow time for feedback and reflection. Every programme was different as they tracked and responded to the developing needs of the organisation and the individuals.

Changing

It is a truism to say that we never get bored with a long-running programme. The reality is that every programme is different. Of course, it is different because of the different mix of people who are participating, but a good programme is also always flexing and responding to the Changing circumstances of the organisation.

The Check here is concerned with the way that the selected development model is able to flex and respond to change. Clearly it must retain resilience in the face of obstacles and should not react unduly to short-term or reaction feedback. The danger of this is that each set of participants goes through the programme that their immediate predecessors would have liked!

But how is the programme geared to handle changes? What are the mechanisms for discussing feedback and managing the response to it? How do we ensure that the programme providers are always up to date with changes inside the organisation?

Snapshot

The consultants providing a senior management programme for a major multinational were treated as non-executive Directors. They received copies of all the Board papers, strategy documents and competitor reports. The organisation argued that 'how else will they continue to be able to really add value?'.

Chronicling

Inherent in all that we are advocating is the contribution to managerial and corporate performance that the management development initiative should be making. Yet we do not want this to be a blind act of faith. We are increasingly moving to the situation where management development is viewed as an investment. Consistent with this view is a need to be clear about the return that the

---

investment is designed to achieve. Equally, however, we must expect to be required to demonstrate in an acceptable manner that the planned returns have actually been delivered!

So as we launch our development initiative, what systems have been designed and put into place to record and document the initiative? There will undoubtedly be benefits that are unanticipated and others that are highly subjective, yet the need remains to measure and check.

Snapshot

The training manager of an international drugs company was quite upset to be told by his Director that the Board wanted to know what had been achieved from their £2million investment in management development. 'I thought that they realised that it was all about long-term education. Now no one can even remember how bad things were when we started - so they see no changes.'

So the final Check in the series is 'have appropriate mechanisms been set up to Chronicle and record the events?'. In discussion recently with a senior banker he was ruing the early retirement programme in his organisation. 'The trouble is that we are losing our corporate memory. We are losing the people who have been through the thinking process that brought us here and there is a danger that we will regress because we can't remember why we did certain things.'

There is also an expression that 'those who fail to learn from history are doomed to relive it'.

Conclusion

In these final two Critical Checks for Construction and Carrying-Out we have focused on the implementation issues associated with our development initiative. We have looked to ensure that the initiative is properly positioned in the hearts and minds of the participants and other interested parties so that it has a fighting chance of success. Finally we have looked at the actions that will be undertaken to maintain the relevance and power of the initiative.

One of the dangers of any new idea or initiative is that it remains as a 'bolt-on extra' to the main activities of the organisation. Or, like the Christmas gift, it is used a few times, then dispatched to the back of the cupboard.

These then are the concerns that we have been addressing in this Chapter. These are the issues that we have invited you to look at within the Checks for Construction and Carrying-Out.

In the next Chapter we will look at where the Wadenhoe Model meshes into your current initiatives and provides a basis for increasing the effectiveness of your management development initiatives no matter what the starting point.

Checklist for Chapter 8

Platform Construction

Has the process of identifying and assembling the Model been carried out in a manner that predicates for a successful launch?

Consultation

- Have you actively canvassed opinion in your organisation about this particular initiative? Have you sought the appropriate involvement from line managers and other interested parties? Do the stakeholders feel that they have been consulted? Have the interested groups been brought together to share their thoughts and ideas?

Communication

- Have people honestly expressed their views and feelings about the proposed development? Have you? Have you clearly conveyed the intentions of the proposed initiative to those involved? Have you explained the proposed actions and their rationale?

Consideration

- Do you feel that you fully understand the concerns of the participants and other interested parties? Have you identified the benefits that each participant or stakeholder will gain from the proposed programme? Do they value the benefits that you have identified?

Comprehension

- Do the managers involved have an overview of the company situation that enables them to put this initiative into perspective? Do they understand the implications for themselves of both taking part in the proposed development and of not taking part?

Commitment

- Do you believe that managers are willing to make the necessary effort to achieve the proposed development and through it to attain the desired performance?

Platform Carrying-Out Checks

Continuity
● Will people in your organisation persevere with the proposed approach? Will the perseverance be consistent across the organisation?

Checking
● What systems and procedures have you put in place to monitor, control and maintain the proposed initiative? How are you proposing to get feedback about the impact of the initiative?

Capturing learning
● Have you instilled an action learning orientation in your organisation? Have the processes and skills for critical reflection and learning from experience been developed and adopted?

Changing
● Is the development model that is being adopted open and amenable to change in response to altered circumstances? Is the approach capable of being modified in accord with developments? Are the means in place for making and holding/consolidating improvements on a continuous basis?

Chronicling
● Have you set up mechanisms for chronicling the events, keeping records and collecting data for logistics and evaluation purposes? Is there a record of the resources used, the participants' reactions, the learning and the outcomes?

Chapter 9
THE MANAGEMENT
DEVELOPMENT LEAGUE

Introduction

In this book we have presented the Wadenhoe Model as a stylised representation of what our research has identified as the critical ingredients of strategically effective management development. We have presented it both in terms of the data that is required for decision-making, and the interactions between the information that needs to be analysed and understood. We have gathered together the best practise that we have observed through many years of working in management development in a form that we believe enables any organisation to improve the effectiveness of its management development thinking and actions; there is always a danger in gathering 'best practice' as a basis for a framework, when what you end up with is bland and featureless.

Snapshot

A few years ago one of the popular magazines asked its readers to identify who they felt were the most attractive men in public life and to specify the single feature that made them attractive. There was a high level of agreement on features like Paul Newman's eyes and Paul McCartney's nose. The magazine then created a photo composite picture that incorporated all of these 'world's most attractive' features into a single face. The result was not unattractive, but it was bland and lacked the power and character that enlightened the original owners.

We believe that the Wadenhoe Model avoids the danger of blandness.

We have therefore tested the framework both in our own work with clients and by inviting management development professionals to debate the Model at each stage in its development. We also run a development programme entitled 'Making Management Development Strategically Effective', which is built around the Wadenhoe Model. We therefore feel confident that the Model is a tool that can be used by any organisation to add to the strategic effectiveness of its management development interventions.

As we have gone through the book describing the Model, the 5P Platform, the Critical Checks and the five Analysis steps, we have also commented on those situations that we have observed where various elements of the Model are miss-ing or 'skewed'; where key information is not available or is not of an acceptable quality; and where information is not tied together in ways that add real focus to our thinking. We have also invited you to examine your own organisation for the ways in which it conforms to the shape and thinking of the Model.

But if we are honest we are also asking you to focus on your deficiencies. And this can be depressing. If by the end of this book we have taken you to a point of saying, 'Yes, this is all very interesting and I can see the logic but there is no way that I can reach that level', then we will have failed.

As we said in an earlier Chapter we have a passionate belief in the ability of people to grow and to develop, so we believe that any organisation can improve the effectiveness of its management development initiatives. The issue is by how much you want to improve or have the resources to achieve.

The focus of this Chapter is to look at organisations that are at different starting points in the sophistication of their management development activities. We want to look at the potential for an organisation to improve the quality of its manage-ment development activities using the Wadenhoe Model, but without necessarily going all the way at the start. We will look at the danger that the effectiveness of an organisation's management development activities could deteriorate over time.

We will introduce the idea of a 'League table' of Management Development sophistication and some ideas of what organisations need to do to get 'promoted', or equally to avoid 'relegation'. We will also look at the idea of a 'cup run' - the organisations that on their day can beat the best. But would they be able to com-pete at that level regularly?

Additionally, we will touch on aspects of the 'Learning Organisation' and the ways in which current thinking matches with the Wadenhoe Model. In the terms of the League concept, is the Learning Organisation emerging as an exciting new force to dominate Premier League thinking? Or is it a giant-killer that is the talk of the terraces for a season or two, then disappears from sight except for a few ardent supporters and believers?

The Management Development League

First let us propose some categorisations for the various Divisions in our Management Development League, then look in more detail at what would be taking place in organisations in each Division with respect to the Wadenhoe Model. Then we will look at the ways in which the Model can help an organisation with the appropriate will and resources to move into the Premier League from any starting point, or alternatively start a process that gradually moves them up through successive Divisions.

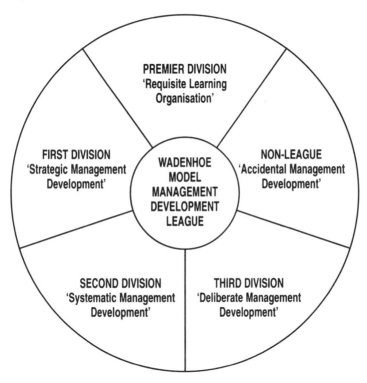

Non-League - Accidental Management Development
At this level we see organisations where Management Development is natural and uncontrived. We see learning occurring as an accidental spin-off from day-to-day work activity. There is no Deliberate Management Development at this level and learning is largely implicit and unfocused.

Third Division - Deliberate Management Development
Here we see explicit, Deliberate and designed learning. However, Management Development activities are isolated, tactical, fragmented and ad hoc. Development is used as a fire-fighting tool dealing with a need here, a need there, as they arise.

Second Division - Systematic Management Development
In the Second Division we observe Management Development that is formalised, planned and co-ordinated. However, the systematic approach often focuses on roles and runs the danger of becoming over-bureaucratic. It may lose its relevance over time, and the systems become ends in themselves.

First Division - Strategic Management Development
Management Development activities here have a business focus. Development initiatives inform, contribute to and in turn implement, support and reinforce strategic business objectives. Nevertheless, Management Development can still be seen as remote and 'ivory tower' in that it appears to be distanced from the reality of the management issues 'on the ground'.

Premier League - Requisite Learning Organisation
In the Premier League responsibility for learning and development is deliberately devolved to individuals who are empowered and facilitated to self-develop on a continuous basis. To achieve Premier League status Management Development needs to be contextually relevant and appropriate in the sense of contributing to the effective achievement of the organisation's strategic objectives.

These then are the broad Divisions of the Management Development League. Again, this is ground that has been covered by other researchers. However, the important issue is, we believe, to understand fully the strengths and weaknesses of being in a particular Division and the costs and benefits to the organisation of trying to move into a different Division.

Let us now look in more detail at what is happening in each Division in terms of the Model and the strengths and weaknesses of that position.

Non-League - Accidental Management Development

These will tend to be organisations where there is no formal management development activity and probably no formal development function. If an HR or personnel function exists it will be focusing on matters of personnel administration (payroll, pensions, sickness, recruitment, etc) without taking any responsibility for management development. Managers working in these organisations will be expected to perform. Any necessary learning is their business and anyway will come about through doing their job. Where they are unable to perform they will be moved into a role where they can be effective, or carried until the organisation finds the burden unacceptable. At this point the organisation will probably bite the bullet and sever the relationship. Budgets for training and development will probably only cover technical matters like export documentation and computer systems.

In the framework of the Model we would identify these organisations as having nothing below the Performance-Development Axis. While above the Axis all of the P elements and the Strategy could be well defined and operationalised, there will be no consideration of Person, Purpose, Process and Place below the Axis.

Thus, for example, it is unlikely that there will be any formal attempts at appraisal, and therefore the identification of development needs and objectives will again be driven by the individual. However, where the individual identifies a development need he/she will need to demonstrate a clear business benefit from the development in order to justify the expenditure. Development Processes will be in terms of courses, and there will be little formal recognition of the manner in which the capabilities of the managers are actually being changed.

The element of Place will be taken as a given - 'this is the way that things are here' - and will depend totally on the leadership style of the Chief Executive as to whether it is a culture that supports performance or development.

In our view there is likely to be no Connections between the P elements that exist. For all this, it has to be recognised that managers in these organisations do develop and the organisations can be strategically effective. We identify the development as *accidental* to differentiate it from *planned*, but it does not imply no development. Where the Chief Executive spends time with his management team talking about the business and his/her view of where the business is going, there is an informal sharing of the strategy. Individuals are expected to draw their own conclusions about the implications of the strategy for the way that they manage, but because of the often close association that the individual feels with the organisation there will be strong personal motivation to serve the organisation well.

In terms of the way that individuals feel ownership of their own development in the light of an understanding of the strategy there are some apparent parallels with the concept of the Learning Organisation that we will examine later.

The movement that is possible up the Management Development League is extensive, depending upon the will and the resources that the organisation is able to put into the Model. Realistically we identify that the distinguishing factor that would move a non-League organisation into the Third Division is an engendering of a sense of Deliberateness in its development activities.

In the context of the Wadenhoe Model this would involve the Deliberate consideration and design-in of the P elements below the Performance-Development Axis. This might involve paying more attention to the P of Performance and linking this to Person and Process. It might still have a dominant focus on the use of courses to achieve development, but it would be recognising the need to make Deliberate attempts at development to meet the performance needs of the organisation.

Third Division - Deliberate Management Development

We defined organisations in this Division as carrying out development that was designed, Deliberate and explicit. However, we also suggested that development activities would be largely tactical and ad hoc in response to particular problems at the individual or departmental level.

Organisations in this Division will see development as a way of solving particular current problems. These may be technical - 'we really need someone to get a grip of our marketing activities' - or managerial - 'he is impossible to work for but we need his technical knowledge; can you get him an interpersonal skills course?'.

Development will usually be seen as an off-site activity with an expectation that the individual will return 'cured'. Although a spot of remedial coaching by the line manager in response to an observed mistake would equally fit into this Third Division, the role of Personnel will often be limited to identifying the right public course.

In the context of the Wadenhoe Model the P elements will be designed-in but on a temporary and fragmented basis. The need for development will often come as a shock to the individual and will be perceived as remedial. The element of Person will be diminished in these organisations, but there will be a strong Performance to Process Connection. Purpose and Place will again tend to be diminished and not Connected into the rest of the elements. The quality of information used for decision-making will be generally subjective.

Having risen above Non-League status, these organisations can both strive for promotion to the Second Division of Management Development or face relegation back to non-League status.

The necessary ingredient for promotion is to make their management development activities Co-ordinated. The threat of relegation would come where development is seen as ineffective or time-consuming (or expensive for what it achieves) and the organisation allows development to 'return to the wild'.

The move to make management development in these organisations Co-ordinated would need to focus on the Connections between Person, Performance and Process. There would be increasing recognition of the Connections within and between the P elements that would be required at different levels in the organisation, and development would tend to be more systematic.

Second Division - Systematic Management Development

Here we are looking at organisations where development is formalised, Co-ordinated and planned.

Whereas in the lower Divisions we anticipated that the Personnel department would be tasked to find a course to solve a particular problem, here we are likely to see the Training Department offering a range of scheduled courses. These courses will often have been tailored to meet an original set of needs defined by the organisation, but will now have become standardised. Attendance on the courses will tend to be ritualistic when people attain a particular level in the organisation or have been in the role for a specified time - middle managers' courses, for example, that are based on having been in a position for five years.

In the terms of the Wadenhoe Model we are seeing the P elements below the Performance-Development Axis become more clearly defined, but with little ongoing responsiveness and strong Connection with the elements above the Axis.

The Ps of Performance and Process will continue to dominate, but with the P of Purpose becoming better understood. The Person element continues to be understated and the Connection with Purpose and Process will focus on the role rather than the individual needs. This can still be effective if the Performance needs of the role are regularly evaluated and modified. The regular and institutionalised approach to development will mean that the Place element is more visible and that development in this way has become part of 'the way we do things around here'. Development is often unquestioned but accepted.

This ritualistic nature of the development approach will often mean that the Strategic Hook is missing or has become lost over time. It probably was visible when a particular programme was conceived, but the programme remains long after the strategic need has moved on. The relevance of the programmes is checked periodically when a new need becomes visible and the Training Department has to respond; this can act as a timely updating for the department of the strategic needs of the business.

Promotion to the First Division of Management Development requires an integration of management development into the elements above the Performance-Development Axis, including the Strategy. In addition, the P of Person needs to be strengthened in terms of recognising the needs of the individual rather than just the role.

Relegation to the Third Division would come from dissatisfaction and frustration with the bureaucracy of management development and a breakdown into more focused if tactical ad hoc needs.

First Division - Strategic Management Development

This is where we see management development activities having a strategic business performance focus. HR professionals will be seeing their role recognised within the business and will be seeking to contribute actively and directly to and support the strategy of the business and its demands on managerial performance.

We would also expect to see the P of Place becoming more openly recognised for its impact both on managerial effectiveness and the willingness of individuals to develop and change. For many it will seem to be a re-emergence of 'the old OD days' while others will be discovering the need to consider all aspects of the environment through an HR strategy.

With the HR function being accepted as an interventionist activity in these organisations, so the Connections, including the cross-braces, will be developed.

As before, these organisations can both strive for promotion and risk relegation. Promotion is to the Premier League where the emphasis is on the Requisite Learning Organisation. The factors engendering promotion are those of empowerment and facilitation of individuals learning while retaining Requisiteness. The learning achieved will be contextually significant in the sense of continuing to contribute to strategic performance achievement. The danger for an organisation in the First Division of Management Development is that the approach to development is still driven centrally. Yet it is becoming increasingly recognised that the competitive environment is changing at an accelerating rate - there are doubts about the ability of a central function to sense the managerial needs and respond to them with a corresponding speed. If this is the case, there is a danger that the development response will always slightly lag behind the required development need. Or alternatively the HR department will be trying to anticipate future needs and may not always get these right. Promotion to the Premier League depends upon finding a way to ensure that the development activities are always sharply focused on the needs that the individual managers recognise as Requisite.

Relegation to the Second Division can come about through bureaucratisation. Here the rate of change of the strategic demands of the organisation leaves the HR function stranded in its inability to respond fast enough. It can then be tempted to fall back on the bureaucracies of appraisal and development needs analysis to identify needs. Or alternatively it can become the guardian of novel forms of development and the development axis again becomes an end in itself (rather than a means to a means to an end).

Premier League - Requisite Learning Organisation

Here we are looking at organisations where responsibility for learning and development is devolved to individuals who are empowered and facilitated to self-develop on a continuous basis.

By implication we are looking at a situation where the Wadenhoe Model not only informs the thinking of the organisation but also the thinking of the individual manager. We see the strategic awareness existing at the level of individual managers who are making use of available objective feedback to determine their own development needs. They will have an understanding of learning that enables a significant amount of development to take place alongside and often instead of formal training programmes, and they will have quality coaching skills to enable others to develop in the workplace.

The HR department will be largely a service function to the managers to facilitate their identified development needs. In addition, they will be actively working with managers to increase the managers' skills of coaching, counselling, performance review and facilitation. The managers themselves will be continuously monitoring the strategic demands of the business to ensure the contextual relevance and appropriateness of their development.

The challenge for the Premier League organisation is to ensure the strategic focus and awareness of its managers. The danger of relegation is twofold. At one level the managers may not acquire a sufficient understanding of their involvement in this self-development approach through lack of time, lack of training or lack of will. The organisation could then find itself in a situation of development returning to being a centralised function as in the First Division organisation.

The alternative danger is that the managers develop in ways that no longer reflect the strategic needs of the organisation; development becomes anarchic and the organisation returns to non-League status.

Engendering promotion up the League	WADENHOE MODEL MANAGEMENT DEVELOPMENT LEAGUE	Avoided relegation down the League
PREMIER DIVISION ↑		**PREMIER DIVISION** ↓
REQUISITENESS ↑		INDIVIDUALISATION DOING OWN THING ↓
FIRST DIVISION ↑		**FIRST DIVISION** ↓
INTEGRATION ↑		BUREAUCRATISATION GOAL DISPLACEMENT ↓
SECOND DIVISION ↑		**SECOND DIVISION** ↓
CO-ORDINATION ↑		FRAGMENTATION AD HOC ↓
THIRD DIVISION ↑		**THIRD DIVISION** ↓
DELIBERATENESS ↑		NATURALISATION 'RETURN TO THE WILD' ↓
NON-LEAGUE		**NON-LEAGUE**

Summary

The Wadenhoe Model helps us to understand the current status of management development in our organisations against an idealised framework of the way that things could be. As with any objective or vision, if we feel that it is too far out of reach we will be de-motivated by the scale of the challenge rather than being motivated to try to achieve an improvement.

In looking at the concept of a 'League table' we have tried to indicate the possible directions and potential for improvement that the Model presents to any organisation irrespective of its starting point. We are not being insensitive and saying, in the words of the joke, 'If I were you I wouldn't be starting from here in the first place'. We are where we are and that is our starting point.

The way that we have presented the Model and the League is intended to convey a number of things:

- It is possible for any organisation to improve the strategic effectiveness of its management development activities by moving up a Division

- Progression is not limited to going up successive Divisions. If an organisation wants to leap directly into the Premier League the Model indicates the processes and the resource implications of attempting this

- Each of the Divisions has a risk of relegation as well as an opportunity for promotion. Management development is in danger if it tries to stand still while the people in the organisation and the competitive environment are changing

- There are costs and benefits of improving the strategic effectiveness of management development.

If you want to go forward we believe that the Wadenhoe Model provides an effective way of doing this.

We started this book by talking about the frustrations that led us to start the research that led to the creation of the Model. We believe that we have gone a long way towards assuaging those doubts and frustrations. We believe that the Model provides the rigour and challenge to our thinking that will enable our management development initiatives to have an impact on the strategic effectiveness of the organisation. Further, we believe that we are increasing the predictability of that impact.

But we have not yet met all our needs.

One of the dreams that we still have is to make the financial link between management development and organisational performance. We believe that the Wadenhoe Model has taken us a considerable way down this road, but there is more to be done.

In the final Chapter we therefore review the next phase of our research programme. This is focusing on 'Putting a Measure on Management Development'.

Chapter 10
PUTTING A MEASURE ON MANAGEMENT DEVELOPMENT

Introduction

We have now looked in detail at the Wadenhoe Model, and in the last Chapter we looked at how the Model may be used to 'raise our game'. Throughout this book our focus has been upon what you need to take account of in formulating management development initiatives that will be strategic and effective in their impact.

In Chapter 8, as part of our consideration of the five Analyses, we prompted you to consider the potential cost benefit of your management development activities. At the same time we are conscious that much work needs to be done if such an Analysis is to be anything more than subjective. Putting a measure on management development by identifying and demonstrating its pay-off is as yet an imprecise science. Indeed, it is more about faith, hope and charity and, it has to be said, prejudice than it is about objective and rational measurement and valuation.

The aim of this Chapter is to focus on these very issues of measuring and evaluating management development. It also serves as a 'coming shortly' for the next major piece of research to be undertaken by The Wadenhoe Centre, which will focus on the issues of valuing and evaluating management development.

At a philosophical level we believe that there is a limit to how much longer we can continue to live with the Human Asset charade! The core of this book is based on recognising the crucial strategic importance of the Human Asset. In many organisations we also see a reawakening of interest in Human Asset accounting. We continue to pontificate about people being our greatest asset, yet management development in many organisations is treated as a cost rather than as an investment in our most important asset. We invest in the maintenance and improvement of our other assets, but still the development of what is acknowledged as our most important asset is considered as a revenue cost. And worse - when times are hard and the budget is under threat, the budgets that are most readily eliminated are considered to be PR, R & D and Training.

We have to recognise that the management development function is at least partly to blame for the situation with its unwillingness or unpreparedness to try and evaluate the impact of its interventions. This is not to say that evaluation is easy, because it clearly is not. Yet we appear to avoid even making attempts to measure the changes that can be measured.

The need to evaluate the impact of any form of management development intervention has always existed. However, the desire to link the achievements of the development directly to the financial results - the 'bottom line' - has driven organisations down narrow tracks of evaluation. The approaches have often foundered on the virtual impossibility of separating the impact of development from other things that have been going on in the organisation. This has led to attempts at evaluation becoming polarised between the 'happiness sheets' that tend to be collected at the end of individual programmes, and the major post-event rationalisations that seek to make causal links to the organisation's bottom-line performance.

We recognise the need to evaluate the impact of management development at a number of different levels, and the purpose of this Chapter is to explore some of these and to identify the work that remains to be done to improve the quality of evaluation.

Levels of Evaluation

Level 1 - Reaction

There will be reactions to any development event. The participants will certainly have reactions, and so also will those who have tutored the event. The reactions will be concerned with:

- the relevance of the content of what they have been through to the participants' perceived development needs

- the timing, pace and level of the event

- the appropriateness of the development process to them and their needs

- the appropriateness of the venue and its environment for the development being undertaken, and

- the tutorial style of the event.

Most competent tutors will be carrying out their own reviews, formally or informally, consciously or unconsciously, during and after the event, but these will be concerned more with immediate issues of content and process.

Level 2 - Learning

The evaluation of the learning that has taken place is likely to be carried out by the participants themselves and therefore is likely to be relatively subjective. Where Development Objectives have been defined there should be the potential to evaluate the extent to which the learning objectives of the event have been achieved.

Unfortunately, experience shows that objectives are often ill or inaccurately defined, or focused on that which can most easily be drafted in the language of an objective rather than reaching the heart of what learning is actually required. Often, too, the learner is not included in the process of formulating objectives for the learning expected. In the event that they are included they are often insufficiently well informed to make a significant contribution to this process.

Whatever the process, the assessment of the learning that has resulted is likely to be left to the discretion of the learner.

Level 3 - Application of learning

In focusing on learning we have yet to consider the issues of the transfer of learning back to the workplace. Unless the spirit of management development is educational and/or personal, we would expect to be concerned with whether or not learning produces changed behaviour in the workplace. Thus the next level of evaluation is concerned with the extent to which the participant has been able to apply the learning in the way intended.

Evaluation of the participant's behaviours should not, however, be restricted to the participant alone. We believe that the evaluation should include the participant's line manager and a cross-section of subordinates; also, in line with current trends these should not be diagonal slices, but 360-degree evaluation involving bosses, peers, subordinates and even outside contractors and customers to test the effectiveness of what they have implemented as well as the progress of the implementation.

If this form of evaluation is to work there is a need for others in the organisation to understand what the learner is trying to implement. This need to share and discuss action plans, especially with the participant's line manager, must be a designed part of the programme with the acceptance and commitment of all parties that this will happen.

Level 4 - Changes to the way that the organisation operates

Management development is rarely done in a spirit of social benevolence. The overall theme of this book is that it is usually undertaken for good business reasons and with the need or desire to change the way that certain things are being done in the organisation in order to make it more effective.

Level 4 in the evaluation process is therefore to examine what has changed in the organisation as a result of the development initiative. Specifically we are looking for the outcomes and impact of managers' changed behaviours in their performance and achievements. Clearly, the further we are removed in time from the actual event the harder it is to make accurate causal links.

Evaluation at this level should, then, have three elements:

- The views of the senior people in the organisation of the 'before' and 'after'

- The views of individuals in the organisation who have sponsored and driven the formal part of the development programme. They will obviously have a view of the problem that the development programme was designed to address and the extent to which it has been successful

- The view of the body of the organisation.

Level 5 - Changes to the organisation in terms of its business outcomes

Ultimately management development is an investment that should be evaluated against the commercial performance of the organisation. If you recall, we identi-fied at the outset that management development was 'a means to a means to an end'; the ultimate end has always been the strategic performance of the organisa-tion. But this level is the most difficult to evaluate. If it is acknowledged that the effects of management development activities on the way that the organisation operates are hard to evaluate, how much harder is it to evaluate the effects at this level, when more variables may have an effect, for example economic conditions, structural changes in the organisation, product development, changes in the mar-ket place, and countless others?

These then are the levels at which we believe a development programme should be evaluated. How does the Wadenhoe Model inform the process of evaluation?

We believe that the fineness of thinking that is at the heart of the Model sub-stantially increases the chance of any management development activity being measured. By making clear at the outset the managerial performance that we are looking to influence we have immediately created a basis for measuring the extent to which any change has occurred. At the levels of reaction, learning, and even behaviour change, we have made explicit the development objectives that the management development initiative is intended to achieve. The develop-ment objectives can provide clear guidelines and criteria against which to judge the impact and the effectiveness of a development activity.

In looking at the Strategic Hook in the Model we have sown the seeds for evaluation at levels 4 and 5, and opened the way for the Cost Benefit Analysis that we described in Chapter 7. We identified at that stage the need to ask senior managers to identify, albeit subjectively, the benefits that they believe would accrue to the organisation if managers were performing in the way and to the standard required.

'Putting a Measure on Management Development'

The steps for evaluation of management development have been well documented in the past and, as we have described above, we believe that the rigour that the Wadenhoe Model demands will add considerably to the quality of information available for evaluation purposes.

However, we recognise that this is not sufficient. In our view there are some significant gaps in the ways that organisations are able to:

● evaluate the real impact that management development has had on the performance of the individual at work, and

● put a value to the organisation on that change in managerial performance.

It is in these two areas that the next stage of The Wadenhoe Centre research programme will be focusing. Just as the Wadenhoe Model has been developed as a framework for organising our thoughts on management development, we now hope to develop a series of frameworks to assist in the process of evaluating the impact of development activities and putting a value on that impact for the organisation.

Clearly, the ideal that we are all seeking is a direct and unequivocal link between an investment in management development and the bottom-line financial performance of the organisation. A perfect cost-benefit correlation would be wonderful.

However, we must again be realistic. In creating the Wadenhoe Model we set out to increase the reliability of our management development interventions. If you remember from the Introduction, our concern was not that management development was a black hole of failure, but that success was insufficiently predictable and reliable for us to be satisfied.

So it is with evaluation and valuing. Through the research we are not aiming to achieve this perfect cost-benefit correlation, because this is an aim that will surely lead to failure. We are concerned to increase the reliability and predictability of the benefits that an organisation is able to recognise from its investment in management development.

Nor at this point are we trying to claim that nothing has been done in this field or that the work that has been done has no value. Indeed, the aim of our research is once again to draw together the work that has been done and the practical experience that has been gained, and to distil this into some practical and pragmatic frameworks that enable us to demonstrate more clearly our intent to make management development a legitimate business investment.

Lest it should be perceived that we are only concerned with the bottom-line performance of management development, we should also identify the need to evaluate the impact of management development.

The analysis above of the various levels of evaluation is a useful starting point without necessarily helping to identify how the evaluation of the impact of management development on managerial performance can actually be achieved.

More work has been done on the impact of formal development events than on other forms of development, but our understanding of Process in the Wadenhoe Model has forced us to recognise the wide range of development actions that are available to us. This aspect of the research is therefore concerned with measuring and evaluating the impact of all forms of development.

The research will be carried out in a consortium of organisations who are keen to work with us in addressing these issues. Starting in the summer of 1995, it will be completed by the end of 1996 and we expect the book of the findings to be published shortly after.

Postscript by Peter D. Hall

Having started this book with a very personal reflection on the frustrations that I was feeling, I ought to close by discussing whether my frustrations have been removed.

I identified in the Preface my concerns that so little had apparently been achieved through management development despite the considerable resources expended. I had a feeling of dishonesty that clients were receiving such a poor return on their investment.

I was embarrassed by the 'hands off' attitude displayed by some of my management development colleagues that distanced them from any involvement in organisational performance. This was combined with a concern that management development was an 'act of faith' for many organisations.

Finally, I was concerned with the focus of more research money being spent on the *topics* of management when I believed that the real problems lay in the *process* of management development.

So am I now content?

Predictably, the answer is 'Yes and no'. I now believe that the application of the Wadenhoe Model as a framework for organising our thinking and decision-making about management development can dramatically increase the likelihood that the development activities will be more focused on the real strategic needs of the organisation.

This is not merely the blind faith of the inventor, but a faith based in real practical experience. We have used the Model in our own interventions with organisations, and we have used it as the basis of our development programme 'Making

Management Development Strategically Effective'. The thinking, the concepts and the constructs of the Model have been rigorously field-tested by some of the most professional industrial organisations, and it has not been found wanting. Indeed, one of the participants on a recent programme remarked that he had worked with a lot of models during the course of his career, and he felt that the Wadenhoe Model was the first that he had encountered that 'retained total integrity even when stripped down to the detail of its individual components'.

I am also content that through this book and through the above-mentioned development programme we have demonstrated that it is possible to create an effective process for contextualising a Generaliseable and Simple framework. In other words we have demonstrated the way in which the user and the researcher can work together to supply the organisational Accuracy.

I have to say that in some ways the Wadenhoe Model has made our lives harder rather than easier. Whereas before we were able to ignore certain issues out of ignorance, we are now acutely aware of what needs to be done to make our interventions as effective as possible. The preparation of development actions is now more demanding, but the results are infinitely more satisfying.

I am also relieved that the research has not come up with some magic 'missing ingredient'. I continue to be concerned with the tendency within the UK to be constantly looking for the 'quick fix'; the 'fad' mentality that has led to the marginalising of many fundamentally good ideas that have not provided instantaneous benefits.

We may sell fewer books because we are not providing a new and novel solution, but professionally I feel more content that we have provided a serious piece of kit to help organisational effectiveness.

I feel content that working through the Wadenhoe Model now prevents management development practitioners from taking a 'hands off' approach. The Model makes explicit the links between management development and real managerial performance at work. Our consideration of Place forces the recognition of those organisational factors that disable managerial performance. And finally, the 'off-line' concept leads us to examine and address issues beyond the bounds of traditional management development thinking, but which have a significant impact on the development activities that should be approved.

Additionally, I feel that the Model makes explicit the thinking and decisions that lie behind management development actions in a way that de-mystifies them. There is no reason for management development to be seen as 'black magic' or for organisations to take it as an act of faith. All of the thinking should be laid bare for the organisation to see and understand.

So why do I also answer 'No' to the question about my frustrations being removed?

Amongst the concerns that I was expressing was one that centred around the 'costs' of management development; the need for organisations to be seeing a return on their investment; and the lack of visibility of the impact of management development on managerial performance. I am not sure that these concerns have really been answered.

We have focused on managerial Performance as one of the cornerstones of the Model, ie one of the P elements of our 5P Platform. But what are the tools and techniques that are available to organisations to help them constantly monitor and evaluate the changes that are occurring in managerial performance? We tend to focus on the evaluation of formal and visible development activities. But what of the informal and opportunistic development? How do we evaluate this? The concept of 'coaching' is once again on everyone's lips. This is clearly a significant development activity with significant cost and resource implications. What frameworks exist to help managers to evaluate the real impact of their training and development activities?

I should hasten to add at this point that I know that frameworks do exist. My concern is with their Generaliseability, Simplicity and Accuracy. Sounds familiar?

I believe that the Wadenhoe Model starts to move us down this route with greater comfort, but I do not believe that we have yet an effective framework or frameworks for doing this.

My greater concern is with the impact of management development activities on the business performance of the organisation, ie on the bottom line. If my earlier concern was a framework for evaluating the impact of management development on managerial performance, my concern here is to make a link in financial terms between managerial performance and the strategic performance of the organisation. How do we put a value on the benefits to the organisation of carrying out management development?

Yes, there are links between some skills areas like selling and the sales volume of the organisation. Or between customer service and customer retention rates. But in the arena of management development the links are poorly established, where they exist at all. Yet as I described in an earlier 'snapshot', one of my clients was able instantly to make the link in his own mind between the managerial performance that he required and the resulting 10 per cent improvement in bottom-line profits.

So what?

At the end of my Preface I asked the rhetorical question: 'If I am so concerned with these issues, what am I going to do about them?'

By the end of 1996 I hope that you will be reading the answer to that question in a book entitled *Putting a Measure on Management Development*. We shall be working with a small consortium of commercial and industrial organisations who will be sharing their thoughts and approaches to these issues, helping us to develop appropriate frameworks and providing us with test sites to validate the frameworks in practice.

We have encouraged you throughout this book to contact us and talk to us about your experiences of using the Wadenhoe Model, and indeed adding to and improving it. Equally, if you have thoughts, ideas or experiences that would contribute to the next phase of the research, we would of course be delighted to hear from you.

Appendix 1
MANAGEMENT DEVELOPMENT - THE CONCEPTS, NOT THE WORDS

Over recent years the number of terms that are used to describe management development and its elements has increased dramatically, leaving people confused and unclear. Manager development? Management development? Personal development? These and many other terms are being used, sometimes loosely and frequently inter-changeably. Do we always know what we mean? And does this matter anyway?

This confusion of language and definitions has serious implications for all of us who are concerned with management development. We know of organisations that are encouraging their managers and other employees to carry out Personal Development Planning. Yet the managements of these organisations have not made their intentions clear about the nature of this development process, and as a result have raised expectations that are not likely to be met.

These are not necessarily expectations of promotion, but also expectations that line managers and others will willingly and enthusiastically contribute to this development process. Confusion in these circumstances has left frustration and cynicism, not good foundations on which to build constructive development processes.

It is not surprising that companies have this problem when even our leading business schools are not clear in which fields of development their programmes are operating. Examine the promotional literature of most business schools and you will find a seemingly random use of terms.

But this lack of clarity and consistency does not rest solely with the providers of courses. Our research shows that companies respond to the providers' brochures without knowing more about the content than what is listed in the short subject headings. More importantly, they make their choices without understanding or questioning the processes that the course delegates will encounter.

From these and other research findings it is clear that there is a need to arrive at some agreed definitions of the various terms being used, to reduce the dangers of misunderstanding. The main phrases whose definitions appear blurred are 'management development', 'career development', 'manager development', 'personal development', 'self-development', 'management training' and 'organisational development'.

There are no universally recognised definitions of these terms., so this paper offers descriptions and considers the practical distinctions between them. This is not just a matter of shuffling words. If a company is to achieve the results that it needs at a cost it is able to afford, it is critically important that it recognises how it is investing its energy and spending its budgets. The *real* differences between these concepts and their consequences therefore need to be understood.

In putting forward these definitions we hope also to stimulate some debate that will lead to a more widespread acceptance of the distinctions between the terms.

Management Development

We use the term 'management development' with the following meaning:

- Planned and deliberate processes to develop the capability of the management of the organisation so that it can meet its strategic requirements both in current performance and in its performance in the future

We are certainly not alone in the way we see this link between strategy and management development. At a briefing for journalists, Alan Sugar was reported as saying that '. . . there are certain things that absolutely must be achieved if the business is to survive, grow and be profitable. The organisational capability to achieve these critical success factors is as a result of the management capability of the firm.'

The former Head of Management Development at British Coal rates management development as '. . . central to the strategic policy of any organisation, be it top corporate or plant. . .'

Current thinking demands a much broader and more strategic view of management development than the educational or training view so often found in the past. The funding of employees to take MBA degrees, sending all managers to a business school for a general management course, training managers in appraisal skills - in our estimation none of these is in itself a 'management development' activity, although it might be if it is part of a planned effort to sustain the strategy of the organisation.

The Department of Management Learning at Lancaster University defines management development as 'A conscious and systematic decision-action process to control the development of managerial resources in the organisation for the achievement of organisational goals and strategies'. This definition hinges on what they mean by managerial resources. If they does not include the infra-structure for the support of the development of managerial capability, we do not feel that this goes far enough.

Management development is not solely concerned with management, training, coaching, mentoring, action learning and so on, ie the mechanisms for learning how to perform as managers. Without appropriate structures, including the ways teams are constituted and used, systems for performance management, reward and control, approaches for identifying and selecting people for management, etc, the learning may not have the opportunity to be transferred and take root in the organisation. These factors constitute the infrastructure for management devel-opment, without which effective development will not take place. Management development must be influenced by and have influence upon the strategy of the organisation. How often is the management trainer actually aware of the compa-ny's strategy? Not often enough, if we are to believe our experiences.

The words 'planned and deliberate' are found in our definition, but the reali-ties of organisational life will mean that there will be much unplanned and less than deliberate activity in practical management development. This should not be excluded, provided that it fits within the overall strategic intention of the organisation. Unplanned, therefore, must not mean unrecognised!

Manager Development

The term 'management development' is often used when what is really being described is 'manager development'. We see this as:

- The individual manager acquiring the management skills, knowledge and outlook necessary for managing effectively

These 'competencies' might be obtained through formal training, but it is also likely that exposure to particular experiences and other less formal methods such as coaching and mentoring will have been influential. Depending on how the individual manager's requirement for learning is determined, this learning could be part of a planned and deliberate management development approach or it might be a random piece of learning with limited relevance to this manager's job in the uniqueness of his own company.

The current thrust for defining management competencies, prompted by the NEDO and BIM/CBI reports in 1987, and carried on by the Management Charter Initiative, seems to us to be chiefly about manager development. Sadly, this is becoming a debate that is taking an academic turn with the consequent clouding of the waters. With his usual refreshing clarity, Gerry Randell of Bradford University Management Centre points out that we have always needed to define in detail the capabilities required for a particular job - for purposes of selection and promotion and for training and development.

This is, in fact, the definition about which so much has been written. Generalisations or confusion between the skill/knowledge and personal attributes required are no more acceptable or of practical value now than they have been in the past.

Personal Development

We contrast 'personal development' with 'manager development'. Personal development is:

- The broader development of the individual, a process that goes on throughout life

The company may or may not choose to give the individual particular aid in furthering personal development.

It is our experience that companies fail specifically to distinguish between personal development and manager development. Because of this, for example, the company may be understandably disappointed when an individual returns from a training event that the company has paid for without any obvious improvement of skills for managing, even though he is now capable of conducting better relationships with his family. One would naturally hope that this ability to improve the quality of family relationships would also transfer to the quality of relationships at work, though there is nothing to ensure that this will automatically be the case.

A recent study of some 400 managers in a wide range of companies produced very diverse concepts of personal development. These ranged from the narrow view that it is the development of skills for present and future posts in the organisation in which the respondent works (in our view, manager development) to the development of the capability of the individual to cope with life in general.

The study also highlights the broad spectrum of ownership of development. This ranges from the willingness of the individual to accept responsibility for personal development through to expecting someone else to take this responsibility - and, in some cases, to pay for it!

Over recent years there has been a trend towards using outdoor activities for development. Indeed, directing staff are often termed Development Trainers.

It is possible for this form of learning event to have either personal or manager development aims depending upon the way tasks and exercises are structured and briefed, and more particularly upon the processes used for review. Too often the decision as to whether the process will focus on personal development rather than manager development will depend upon the trainers' values and perspectives, which could be different from those held by the delegates or the company that is sponsoring them. Sadly, too many organisations have dipped their managers' toes into this hot water without recognising the possible outcomes for the company or the individuals.

Career Development

We see this as a particular focus of 'personal development', which is about preparing for the pursuit of earning a living. Where some may want to include elements of life planning in their approach to 'career development', we regard this as the broader 'personal development'. We use the term 'career development' to mean:

● Planning and developing the acquisition of the experience, skills and knowledge needed for progress, lateral movement or change of direction in the realm of work

It goes without saying that these days this is not necessarily with the same company! Nor is this likely to change in the future, though a burning issue for some technologically advanced companies is how to persuade employees who have gained substantial experience to see out their career with them, thus ploughing back in the fruits of their experience.

Career development takes on a new meaning in those organisations where structures have flattened, removing traditional career paths. There is a substantial body of knowledge about individual motivation and it seems to us that this is relevant to this problem.

The whole area of careers and career development is massive. As a field it has been heavily researched, but much of this has been in respect of the school leaver and from the point of view of the individual, begging the question of what the organisation can do. As guidance on this, we select one concept - that of 'career anchors' by Edgar Schein - as a starting point. Anyone responsible for considering the development of people in their organisations will find this of value.

Management Development and Management Training

From these definitions it is now possible to examine further confusion in the ways that development takes place.

The purpose of management training is to develop the skills and, as importantly, the outlook for managing effectively. As we have seen earlier, the trend to define competencies across the board is one basis for defining management education and training needs. But will this broad brushstroke apply to the particular requirements of your company, or is something more specific or different needed?

In some organisations line managers are being encouraged to take more responsibility for the training of their subordinates. We support wholeheartedly the need for line managers to be fully involved practically and emotionally in the development of their employees. But there must be monitoring at a strategic level of what is going on in the name of management development in the company. This is often the missing link.

In some cases, leaving management training to the line manager has led to what can be termed the 'mail order catalogue' approach to management development, ie a scanning of courses and picking out those that meet the fancy.

The college, business school or training company providing courses is not likely to be fully committed to meeting the management development needs of the organisation. They are in the business of providing courses rather than developing the management of all the companies for whom they offer course places. This is exemplified by a professor in a business school who has declared that he is not concerned with what happens beyond the lecture room. The prime motive for offering courses, even in the most august institutions, is likely to be to fill available capacity. The extent to which real learning and development will take place will depend upon the zeal and values of the individual lecturer. Even then, he or she will be severely constrained by the academic conditions of service.

Self-Development

Like 'personal development', this has become a much-used term. For us, self-development is one of many methods for generating learning where the individual takes responsibility for the learning aims and objectives and for meeting them. Consequently, self-development approaches can be used for manager development, career development and the wider personal development discussed earlier.

Thirty years ago Peter Drucker was reminding us that all development is self-development. His concept was that no one else can develop another person, but he added, significantly, that it was the responsibility of management to create the conditions in which individuals would want to develop themselves. We agree strongly with this. We know from our experience that the idea of self-development has been grasped by some organisations because it is seen as a cheap option. For many it is a far from easy option, and as work in Esso has shown, there is a need for well-structured support for effective self-development.

Management Development and Organisational Development

'Organisational development' means very different things, depending on whose work you read or who you talk to, but a common basis for most of the approaches is the management of large-scale change using the behavioural sciences. The distinctions between management development and organisational development are now more blurred than ever. They were never very clear in any case. William Bridges puts his finger on why organisational development failed to fulfil its glittering promises.

'Much that passes,' he says, 'for organisational development is little more than organisational repair. In fact there are only two kinds of activities that deserve to be called organisational development.'

'The first is the activity of unfolding the inherent potentialities of the organisation's basic character and compensating for its weaknesses so that those potentialities can be realised. The second is the activity of helping the organisation to move through the natural phases of growth so that it can bear the fruit of its maturity.'

We see that the purpose of much of today's management development - as we defined it earlier in this paper - is to bring about these types of change within the organisation. We can, therefore, only see management development and organisational development as so closely aimed at similar purposes as to make the practical distinction between them hardly worthwhile.

The natural successor to organisational development can be found in the attempts to create 'Learning Organisations'. This can be a woolly concept, but the collective wisdom indicates 'an organisation that facilitates the learning of all its members and *transforms* itself'. Peter Senge's view of a learning organisation is a group of people continually enhancing their capacity to create what they want to create.

The concept of a learning organisation is too important to deal with briefly in this paper. We shall therefore make this the subject of one of our future papers.

The Future - Continuous Learning?

Our final thoughts in this paper are prompted by Peter Wickens, Personnel Director of Nissan. He argues that with today's flattened organisations many of the tasks traditionally regarded as the prerogative of the manager are now being carried out by non-managers. Consequently, continuous development for all employees is necessary rather than a pure management development focus.

This could mean a monumental leap for industry and commerce in the UK where many companies have not even managed purposeful management development. For those in this category we suggest revisiting our definition of management development.

First published in March 1993 as a Wadenhoe Centre Occasional Paper.

Appendix 2
COMPETENCE DOMAINS

'What you need to be mindful of'

Seven areas of performance activity requiring a focus of attention by the top team:

- **Overarching:** Strategic success factors and their integration and co-ordination in the business:
    competitive advantage
    profitablility
    strategic vision, goals and plans
    pattern and balance of risks and reward
    effectiveness of the top team and its leadership
    capability and alignment of the people

- **Market place:** The company's sales and marketing effort.

- **Control:** The control of finances, efficiency and quality in the company

- and **Organisation:** The organisation of operational tasks and processes in the company.

- **Technology:** The company's focus on technological innovation and excellence in its products and processes.

- **Human resources:** The capability and utilisation of the company's employees.

- **Inputs:** The company's supply of materials, services, equipment, advice, information, etc.